MW01644379

Breaking the Bell

Breaking the Bell

The Educator's Guide to
EARNING WHAT YOU'RE WORTH WHILE DOING WHAT YOU LOVE

Manuel Ferrer, Ed.D.

FIRST EDITION

Breaking the Bell

The Educator's Guide to Earning What You're Worth While Doing What You Love

Printed in the United States of America

First Edition

ISBN 979-8-9985217-0-6 paperback
ISBN 979-8-9985217-1-3 case laminate
ISBN 979-8-9985217-2-0 ebook
Library of Congress Control Number: 2025906927

Cover and Interior Design by:
Chris Treccani

Created with the Book to Millions® Method

BOOK BONUSES

Included with your purchase of *Breaking the Bell* are several Book Bonuses which include

- Worksheets
- Training Videos
- Personal Blueprint
- Additional Resources

As a former educator, I know how important it is to immediately take action on what you have learned.

This book is meant to be your blueprint. Utilizing the additional resources provided will set you up to maximize your experience as you Break the Bell and transition into your Next Chapter.

BreakingTheBell.com/Resources

DEDICATION

To my wife, Maria—my life partner, my anchor, and the unwavering believer in every leap I've taken. Your love has been my foundation, especially when the ground beneath me was uncertain. Thank you for giving me the strength—and the space—to break the bells that once held me back.

To my daughters, Alyssa and Bryanna—may this book remind you that freedom lives on the other side of fear. Never doubt the power of your voice, your dreams, or your right to leap. And may you always feel permission to break any bell that stands between you and your fullest potential.

To every educator who's ever felt called to more—this is for you.

TABLE OF CONTENTS

NOTE TO THE READER

At the time of writing this book, I had reached a pivotal stage in my life where work was no longer about earning a paycheck but about fulfilling my passion for education. I realize this is a luxury not afforded to everyone, and I approach this acknowledgment with humility and deep gratitude. For many of you reading this, the reality may feel very different—perhaps you feel trapped, undervalued, or unseen in your current position. This book is for you. It's for anyone who has ever wondered if there is more out there for them but has felt paralyzed by fear, uncertainty, or a sense of loyalty to a system that no longer serves them. My message to you is this: If not now, when?

The journey to this moment has been anything but smooth. In fact, the decision to write this book came during an abrupt separation from my most recent employer—the fourth such departure in two years. Despite my experience and success, I found myself in a pattern of seeking positions that never quite fit. Each opportunity seemed promising at first, but I quickly realized that none of them aligned with my personal and professional values. Long ago, dating back to my days as a school administrator I made a firm decision that I would never again trade one master for another. I was done working for leaders, companies, or organizations that didn't fulfill me personally and professionally. I committed to myself that if I worked, it would be on my own terms.

During the three-month period of reflection that followed my last professional separation, I made another commitment: to write this book. I wanted to share my journey and help other educators who, like me, have felt underappreciated and overlooked. This book is for those of you who feel stuck in a system that doesn't appreciate your unique talents, creativity, or ability to impact lives. It's for anyone who has ever dared to dream of a career beyond the confines of the traditional education system, whether in the private sector or as an entrepreneur.

The title, *Breaking the Bell,* represents more than just a catchy phrase; it's a call to action. For centuries, the school bell has symbolized order, discipline, and control. It dictates when students should move, learn, and even dream. But for many educators, the bell's rings have become a metaphor for confinement—a rigid system that dictates how you should work, live, and measure your worth. In this book, I encourage you to break that bell—to shatter the paradigms that have kept you tethered to roles that no longer fulfill you.

Let's be clear: this isn't about abandoning education or diminishing the vital role of teachers and schools. On the contrary, I firmly believe in the transformative power of education and the need for exceptional educators in classrooms around the world. What I advocate for is your right to earn what you're worth while doing what you love, whether that means staying in education, transitioning into the private sector, or starting your own venture. Your skills are invaluable, and your impact can extend far beyond the walls of a school.

This book is both a memoir and a guide—a hybrid structure designed to inspire and equip you to take the leap. I'll share my story, from growing up in poverty in Little Havana to becoming the first member of my family to attend college. I'll recount my transition from teacher to entrepreneur and beyond, including the missteps, heartbreaks, and triumphs that have shaped my journey. I'll also provide practical tools and frameworks, such as The Next Chapter™ system and the 4-L Framework (Learn, Lead, Leverage, Launch), to help you navigate your own path.

Ultimately, this book is about freedom—freedom to define your worth, pursue your passions, and create a life that aligns with your values. It's about breaking free from the conditioning that tells us we must remain where we are, even when we feel called to do more. It's about choosing courage over comfort, action over complacency, and purpose over paycheck.

As you read this book, I invite you to reflect on your own journey. Where are you now? What's holding you back? And most importantly, where do you want to go? My hope is that *Breaking the Bell will not only inspire you* but also equip you to take that first step toward the life you've been dreaming of.

Remember, the bell that has held you in place doesn't have to define your future. You have the power to break it. And when you do, you'll discover a world of opportunities waiting for you to seize.

If not now, when?

INTRODUCTION TO BREAKING THE BELL

Who This Book Is For

Breaking the Bell is for educators who feel the call for something more. If you've ever felt undervalued, financially strained, or stuck in a system that doesn't fully reward your dedication, this book is your roadmap to a new future. Whether you're a teacher seeking new career opportunities, an administrator exploring leadership roles beyond traditional education, or an educational professional—such as a counselor, physical or occupational therapist, athletic coach, or art teacher—looking for financial independence, this book is your roadmap. The "Extended Educator" section in each chapter ensures that no matter your role, you'll find tailored strategies to help you transition into sales, entrepreneurship, and beyond. With practical insights and actionable steps, you'll gain the confidence, knowledge, and tools to break free from limitations and create a fulfilling, financially rewarding career on your terms.

This book is also for those who have already started their journey but need a proven system to break through obstacles and accelerate their success. If you've ever wondered how your skills in education translate into business, sales, or leadership, you're in the right place.

Breaking the Bell provides the tools, frameworks, and inspiration to help you take control of your career and financial destiny.

How to Use This Book

Breaking the Bell is designed not just as a book, but as a strategic guide—a blueprint for transforming your skills and experience into lucrative opportunities beyond the classroom. It's structured to help you move through the transition at your own pace while providing actionable steps at each stage of your journey.

Each chapter is built around practical strategies, personal stories, and interactive exercises that will challenge you to reflect, take action, and build momentum. This book isn't just about reading—it's about doing.

As you read, use the reflection prompts and exercises to identify where you are in your journey. Take notes, highlight key sections, and revisit the chapters that resonate most with your current challenges and goals.

Additionally, this book is designed to be referenced repeatedly. You'll find yourself coming back to different sections as you progress, using it as a manual for growth. Each chapter is a stepping stone, helping you break free from limiting beliefs, identify opportunities, and execute a plan for success.

At the end of each chapter, we include a "Next Chapter, New Challenge" section—a recap of what you just read and how it connects to the next step in your journey. This section serves as a bridge between concepts, helping you reflect on key takeaways and prepare for what's ahead. Use this section to reinforce your learning, take action on suggested exercises, and set the stage for the next phase of your transformation.

How Each Chapter Will Guide You

Breaking the Bell is structured into three parts, each representing a crucial stage in your transformation.

Part 1: The Opening Bell—My Journey from Educator to Entrepreneur

The opening bell signals the start of something new. In this section, I share my personal journey from being an educator to becoming a successful entrepreneur and sales professional. You'll see the pivotal moments that shaped my decision to transition, and you'll gain insights into how to recognize your own calling for change.

- **Chapter 1:** Awakening to Opportunity - The Moment Everything Changed
  Understand the signs that indicate it's time for a change and how to embrace new possibilities.

- **Chapter 2:** From Educator to Embarker to Entrepreneur - Embracing a Growth Mindset
  Learn how mindset shifts can unlock doors and prepare you for success beyond the classroom.

- **Chapter 3:** Endings, New Beginnings - Burning the Ships
  Discover why fully committing to your transition is the key to long-term success.

Part 2: Answering the Bell - The Call for Change

This section explores the deeper motivations behind your desire for change and introduces frameworks to help you navigate the transition successfully.

- **Chapter 4:** Embrace the Future – If Not Now, When?
  Explore why delaying change is costing you time, money, and personal fulfillment.

- **Chapter 5:** The Three Personas – Educator, Embarker, Entrepreneur
  Identify where you are in your journey and what steps you need to take to move forward.

- **Chapter 6:** Navigating the Transition with the 4-L Framework – Learn, Lead, Leverage, Launch
  A step-by-step process to help you smoothly transition from the classroom to a successful career in sales and entrepreneurship.

Part 3: Breaking the Bell—Your Next Chapter in Business and Beyond

This final section is your launchpad into a new career and financial freedom. Here, you'll learn proven strategies to build your brand, secure opportunities, and create a sustainable side hustle, career shift, or entrepreneurial path that aligns with your values.

- **Chapter 7:** Seize the Moment – Adopting the Entrepreneur Mindset for Success
  Cultivate the mindset needed to thrive in your next chapter—whether it's launching a side hustle, joining a mission-driven organization, or stepping into entrepreneurship.

- **Chapter 8:** The F.R.E.E.D.O.M. Formula – Unlocking Your Path to Financial Independence
  Learn the powerful framework for creating a fulfilling and financially freeing path—whether that's through a side hustle, a new career, or building your own business.

- **Chapter 9:** The Final Bell – A Call to Action
  Your final push to step fully into your new role, with actionable next steps to ensure your continued success.

JOIN THE BREAKING THE BELL™ COMMUNITY

Breaking the Bell™ isn't just a book—it's a blueprint for real change, backed by a supportive community of educators rewriting what's possible. By joining our community, you'll connect with like-minded educators who are transforming their skills into income, impact, and independence.

Here's how you can get involved:

1. Visit www.BreakingTheBell.com: Gain access to additional resources, exercises, and training materials to support your journey.
2. Join the Breaking the Bell™ Facebook Group: Connect with others making the transition, share insights, and get real-time advice.
3. Follow our YouTube channel—@drmanuelferrer: Watch content designed to help you grow and succeed in your new career.
4. Follow us on X (formerly Twitter)—@drmferrer and @ breakingdbell: Stay updated with insights, tips, and community conversations.
5. Sign up for the The Next Chapter™– Educator Career Transition: A structured training program designed to help educators exploring side hustles, interested in corpo-

rate and non-profit organizations, or starting a business of their own.

Book a One-on-One Strategy Session: Work directly with a mentor who understands your background and can guide you step-by-step. Email us to book your strategy session at: Book@BreakingTheBell.com. You are not alone on this journey. There is a whole network of educators who have successfully made the transition and are thriving. It's time to break the bell, take control of your future, and build a career that gives you the financial freedom and fulfillment you deserve.

PART 1:

The Opening Bell— My Journey from Educator to Entrepreneur

CHAPTER 1:

Awakening to Opportunity – The Moment Everything Changed

The "opening bell" is a symbol of fresh starts and endless possibilities. For some, it signals the start of trading on Wall Street; for others, it marks the first day of a new school year. For me, the opening bell signifies those transformative moments in life when everything shifts, when you make a choice to step into something bigger. My journey has been defined by such moments— each one a call to embrace change and see opportunity where others might only see obstacles.

Growing up in Little Havana during the 1990s crack epidemic, life was anything but easy. Our neighborhood was overrun with addiction, poverty, and violence. Stability was a luxury we couldn't afford, and the weight of those circumstances often felt unbearable. My parents weren't around, so my maternal grandmother took on the responsibility of raising me. Despite the crushing reality of our situation, she was a lighthouse of resilience, doing everything in her power to create opportunities for me.

In the midst of chaos, school became my refuge. Every morning, when that school bell rang, it felt like a lifeline—a chance to escape the turmoil and step into a space where hope was still alive. The classroom wasn't just a place to learn; it was a sanctuary, a place where I could dream. My teachers, books, and the power of learning became tools I used to carve out a path beyond the circumstances I was born into.

For many educators like you, the classroom isn't just where you teach; it's where you inspire, protect, and empower. I know this because I've been in your shoes. Like me, you may see the potential in your students that others overlook. You may spend nights rethinking lesson plans to meet their unique needs or wondering how you can reach that one student who seems unreachable. You give your all because you believe in the power of education to change lives. But let me ask you: when was the last time you invested in your own dreams?

My love for reading was one of the first sparks that lit the way. Books offered an escape, a sense of control, and a glimpse into worlds beyond my own. They also planted the seed of something greater—a belief that education wasn't just a tool for survival but a stepping stone to transformation.

Still, the challenges of poverty were ever present. I remember nights in the sweltering heat of South Florida with no air conditioning, lying awake as the humidity clung to everything. Dinner often consisted of instant mashed potatoes, a staple because it was cheap and easy to stretch. I watched my grandmother haggle with the owner of the local bodega for discounts on dented cans, carefully calculating every penny to make sure we had enough to get by. Despite these struggles, her unwavering love and determination shone through. Even in the hardest moments, she taught me the power of grit, sacrifice, and resourcefulness—lessons that would shape me for the rest of my life.

Those lessons stayed with me. They became the foundation for how I approached my career as an educator and, later, as an entrepreneur. The first step to transformation is recognizing that opportunity often comes disguised as hardship. And for me, that recognition started with the sound of the school bell and the courage to answer its call.

For you, that "opening bell" moment might look different. It could be the day you realized the classroom wasn't your only avenue to make an impact. Or perhaps it was a quiet moment of reflection after yet another sleepless night, wondering how to make ends meet. Maybe it was seeing your students struggle and imagining a way to help them beyond the four walls of your classroom. Whatever your moment is, it's calling you to step out of your comfort zone and into something bigger.

In this chapter, we'll explore how to recognize your own "opening bell" moments—those turning points that challenge you to step out of your comfort zone and embrace the unknown. Whether they're born from adversity, inspiration, or pure necessity, these moments can be the catalyst for extraordinary change. Let's start by identifying those moments in your life and reflecting on how they've shaped who you are today.

From Scarcity to Growth

The hardships of my youth didn't just shape me—they became the fuel for my determination to break free. Poverty wasn't just a challenge; it was a constant presence that reminded me of what I didn't have and what I desperately wanted to change. At times, it made me angry—angry at the circumstances, and at the way life seemed stacked against people like me. But that anger became my fire. It pushed me to prove that I was more than my environment, more than my struggles.

From this journey, I developed what I now call the "3 Ps Framework": Poor, Pissed-Off, and Proud.

- **Poor:** I grew up knowing the weight of financial scarcity—the kind that teaches you to make do with little and stretch every resource to its limit. But instead of letting it defeat me, poverty gave me a hunger for something better, a vision for a life beyond what I could see around me.
- **Pissed-Off:** The frustration I felt wasn't just a passing emotion—it was a spark. It lit the fire that drove me to act, to fight for a different future, and to push past every obstacle that tried to keep me in place. I turned my anger into energy, refusing to settle for what the world said I was allowed to have.
- **Proud:** Through it all, I took pride in my resilience. Every achievement, no matter how small, became a victory. Each step forward was proof that I could rise above my circumstances. That pride wasn't about ego; it was about honoring the sacrifices my grandmother made and the determination it took to keep going.

This framework wasn't something I learned from a book or a seminar—it came from life itself. It's a mindset that helped me move from a place of scarcity to a mindset of growth, where I could see challenges not as barriers but as opportunities to rise.

As educators, we know what it means to persevere, to fight for something greater, even when the odds are stacked against us. The "3 Ps" are a reminder that no matter where we start, we have the power to transform our circumstances—and ourselves. Let this be your call to embrace your fire and step into a future where possibility is limitless.

The Educator's Journey

Teaching wasn't just a career—it was a calling rooted in the heart of my community. When I became a teacher, it wasn't just about stepping into a classroom; it was about returning to the very middle school that had shaped me. Walking those hallways, now as an educator, felt like coming home. Every corner of the building held memories—the struggles, the small victories, the teachers who had believed in me when I couldn't yet believe in myself. This school wasn't just where I taught; it was a reflection of my community—students, families, and neighbors who shared the same streets and stories that had shaped my own.

My mission was more than delivering lessons; it was about inspiring hope and showing what was possible. That dedication earned me recognition as Rookie Teacher of the Year, and six years later, Teacher of the Year. These honors weren't just titles—they validated my commitment to changing lives.

But the challenges grew. As an Assistant Principal, I balanced administrative demands, adjunct teaching, and raising twin toddlers with my wife, who was on maternity leave. Despite my achievements, our family struggled financially, living paycheck to paycheck in a cramped townhouse. It was a sobering reminder that, despite breaking the cycle of poverty, I hadn't escaped its grip entirely.

This realization wasn't the end of my passion for education. Instead, it marked the beginning of a new chapter—a journey to make a greater impact and secure my family's future. It was the turning point where I reimagined what was possible, not just as an educator, but as an entrepreneur.

Embracing Change

The first bell I answered wasn't the metaphorical kind—it was the distinct ring of an old rotary phone sitting on my desk. It was late in the day, and I was finishing up paperwork in my office. The school hallways were quiet, and as the phone rang, I glanced at the clock. Part of me thought about letting it go, eager to head home to my baby girls after a long day.

But that wasn't who I was. No matter how exhausted I felt, I always answered. It didn't matter if I was running on fumes-if that phone rang this late, it had to be serious. Maybe one of my teachers needed me. Maybe a student was in trouble. So, I picked it up. On the other end was a voice with a southern drawl, saying, "I'm calling to see if you know any administrators who might be interested in exploring a role in sales we have open."

Without missing a beat, and sensing this might be my moment, I replied, "Stop calling. You found your guy."

That conversation marked the unexpected start of my journey into the private sector, joining one of the largest textbook publishing companies in the world. It was a leap I hadn't planned, but it felt like fate, just as it had when I returned to teach at the very same middle school I once attended. This call wasn't just a job offer; it was a signal. A turning point. A reminder that sometimes, opportunity doesn't knock—it rings on an old rotary phone. Stepping into the corporate world wasn't easy. It felt like I was walking away from a calling. But the same resilience that carried me through my toughest years rose up again - only this time, I wasn't just fighting to survive. I was fighting to grow, to build stability, and to create a future where my family could thrive. That move, first as a Sales Executive and later as an entrepreneur, changed everything. It wasn't just a career pivot. It was a transformation. I discovered that the very skills and passion that fueled my work in education could unlock opportunities far beyond the classroom—opportunities that offered both impact and financial freedom.

A New Chapter, A Renewed Mission

As I stepped into this new chapter, the 3 Ps—Poor, Pissed-Off, and Proud—came full circle. Poverty and anger had been the fuel that set me on this path, but now pride was the dominant force. I was proud of what I had accomplished and the lives I was impacting through my work. Most importantly, I had broken the cycle of poverty that had overshadowed my early years.

This shift didn't come without challenges. The transition tested me in ways I hadn't anticipated, forcing me to step out of the familiar and into the unknown. But every challenge reinforced the lessons I'd learned throughout my life: the importance of resilience, adaptability, and the courage to bet on yourself.

Your Opening Bell

Throughout this book, I'll guide you to recognize your own pivotal moments—the turning points that quietly invite transformation. These moments rarely announce themselves with clarity. Instead, they show up as friction, disguised as detours or disguised opportunities. Often uncomfortable, sometimes inconvenient, they nudge you toward growth by pulling you away from the familiar. Stepping into the unknown will challenge you, but it will also reveal parts of yourself that only emerge under pressure. Each chapter is designed to help you spot these crossroads in your own life and shift your mindset from hesitation to possibility. Because the truth is, change doesn't wait for permission—and neither should you. My hope is that, through my story, you'll begin to see your own defining moments more clearly. Whether they come as setbacks, whispers of opportunity, or full-on disruptions, they carry the potential to reshape your life. Like the bell that once signaled the start of a school day, these moments mark not an end—but a beginning. The question is: will you step forward when the moment calls? Your circumstances, no matter how daunting, don't define your potential. Each of us has the capacity to rise, to grow, and to embrace change. It's time to answer your own call and step into the possibilities that await. You don't need a perfect plan—just the courage to begin. The truth is, most breakthroughs start as quiet nudges: a restless feeling, a passing thought, a door you didn't expect to open. What you do next is what matters. Because growth doesn't come from staying where it's comfortable. It comes from trusting that you're capable of more, and being bold enough to prove it to yourself. The chapters ahead will give you the tools, the mindset, and the roadmap. But the leap? That's yours to take.

Let's begin.

The 3 Ps Framework guided me through every step:

- Poor reminded me of where I started and why change was essential.
- Pissed-Off motivated me to challenge the status quo.
- Proud empowered me to keep striving for more.

EXTENDED EDUCATOR

The Door Was Always There

If you're a school counselor, coach, therapist, SLP, or administrator, I want to talk to the part of you that's been wondering, "*Is there's more for me out there?*"

You've spent your career pouring into others—organizing crisis plans, leading IEPs, managing a hundred moving parts before most people finish their coffee. But somewhere along the way, that whisper begins to creep in—and get's a little louder with each passing school year.

This chapter isn't just about seeing opportunity—it's about admitting that you deserve one too.

And it doesn't need to be dramatic. That first step might be starting a podcast for young athletes, building a trauma-informed workshop for your district, or turning your SEL expertise into something bigger than one school.

You don't need permission. The door was always there. You just finally noticed it.

Mini-Win:

Identify which of the 3 Ps reflects your mindset today and how you can begin breaking your own bell of limitation:

1. **Poor:** You might feel like you're stuck in a rut, struggling financially, and unsure how to break free.
2. **Pissed-Off:** Maybe you're frustrated with your current situation—tired of the same routine, fed up with the limitations, and ready for something more.
3. **Proud:** You take pride in what you've achieved but feel there's more out there for you.

Breaking the bell isn't about abandoning everything you know; it's about recognizing when it's time to step into discomfort and embrace growth. Each of these mindsets—whether born from scarcity, frustration, or ambition—holds the power to drive meaningful change in your life.

Now that you've identified where you stand, the next step is clarity. Breaking free begins with understanding the limiting beliefs tied to your mindset and redefining the path ahead. Growth starts when you challenge those limitations and make the decision to act boldly. Let's explore how shifting your perspective can unlock the opportunities waiting for you.

Reflection:

List three significant events or moments in your life that have left a lasting impact on you (e.g., challenges, achievements, or transitions).

- Event 1:
- Event 2:
- Event 3:

Why were these moments pivotal?

Next Chapter, New Challenge: Embracing a Growth Mindset

Recognizing the opportunity for change is only the first step. The real transformation begins with a mindset shift—a willingness to let go of what's comfortable and take bold action toward the unknown. In this chapter, we'll explore how to reimagine your skills and embrace a growth mindset, setting you on a path toward meaningful change.

CHAPTER 2:

From Educator to Embarker to Entrepreneur – Embracing a Growth Mindset

The sound of the school bell has always been more than just a signal to start the day. For many educators, it's a reminder to show up, face challenges, and persist through adversity. But what happens when the bell rings differently—when it's no longer just a call to teach but a call to transform? This moment isn't about abandoning your passion for education; it's about recognizing that your skills and experiences can carry you beyond the boundaries of what feels familiar.

Shifting into a growth mindset starts with reframing how you see yourself and your potential. A growth mindset isn't just a belief that you can learn and evolve; it's the conviction that stepping into discomfort is where true growth happens. This shift doesn't happen overnight. It takes courage to confront the fears that hold you back. Questions like, "Will my skills translate?" or "What if I fail?" are natural, but they shouldn't define your journey.

Here's what you need to know: the same traits that make you successful as an educator— adaptability, resilience, creativity, and the ability to inspire others—are the very traits that can propel you forward in new and exciting ways. You're not starting over; you're building on a solid foundation, reimagining how those strengths can serve you in a different context.

Imagine your skills as tools:

- **Communication and Influence:** You know how to break down complex ideas and inspire action. This is invaluable in any field.
- **Problem-Solving:** You've navigated challenges in real-time, from managing a classroom to solving organizational issues.
- **Strategic Thinking:** You've planned lessons, projects, and goals with long-term impact in mind.
- **Leadership:** You've motivated students, colleagues, and teams to achieve success together.

When you start to view your experiences through this lens, opportunities become clearer. Your background in education isn't a limitation; it's your unique advantage. Those skills that transformed lives in the classroom can now be the foundation for something bigger—a career path that offers both fulfillment and freedom.

This chapter is your call to action. The bell is ringing again, but this time it's calling you to step out of your comfort zone and embrace the possibility of transformation. Let's reimagine your skills, confront your fears, and build the mindset that will guide you to what's next. True growth begins when you choose to answer the call.

The Breaking Point

You love being an educator. You take pride in your work—the lessons you deliver, the lives you shape, the countless hours spent ensuring your students feel seen, heard, and inspired. But somewhere along the way, you begin to feel the weight of it all. The late nights grading papers, the weekends spent preparing for the next week's challenges, and the extra responsibilities you take on without hesitation. Despite your unwavering dedication, there's a growing disconnect between your efforts and the life you've envisioned for yourself.

Maybe you've been here: juggling a household budget that always feels just a little too tight. Stretching every dollar and sacrificing to ensure your family's needs are met, all while pushing down that gnawing sense of frustration. You give your heart to your work, yet the financial strain remains a constant reminder that something isn't adding up. The accolades, the years of experience, even the advanced degrees—none of it seems to make the difference you thought it would.

And then comes a moment that stops you in your tracks. Maybe it's a bill you weren't expecting, an opportunity you can't afford to seize, or the realization that no matter how hard you work, the numbers just don't add up. For me, it was a tax-filing moment that forced me to confront a harsh truth: my best efforts, as much as I loved what I did, weren't enough to create the life I wanted for my family.

That moment of realization doesn't have to be the end—it can be the beginning. Sometimes, breaking points are what push us to reevaluate, to step back and ask: What if there's something more? What if the skills, resilience, and passion that have carried me this far could be used in a way that offers not just fulfillment, but freedom?

Stepping into the unknown isn't easy. It's uncomfortable, even frightening. But it's also the space where growth happens. When I realized something had to change, I didn't have all the answers. What I did have was a willingness to act. To take the skills I'd honed as a teacher, a mentor, and a leader, and reimagine how they could create new opportunities for me and my family.

This isn't the end of your story as an educator; it's the beginning of something bigger. The lessons you've learned in the classroom—how to inspire, adapt, and persevere—can carry you into new and exciting possibilities. Whether it's starting your own venture, transitioning to a new field, or finding a way to redefine your path, you have everything you need to rise to the challenge.

Your breaking point isn't a failure; it's a signal. A call to stop, reassess, and make bold decisions about what's next. Because sometimes, when it feels like you're breaking, you're actually breaking free.

In the chapters ahead, we'll explore how to recognize these moments of transformation and turn them into opportunities. It's not easy, but it's worth it. Let's take this journey together and see what happens when you answer your own call.

Recognizing the Need for a Growth Mindset

A growth mindset isn't just a buzzword—it's a necessity for anyone looking to transform their life. It's the belief that challenges are opportunities waiting to be conquered, that effort leads to growth, and that failure is simply a stepping stone to success. For me, embracing this mindset wasn't optional—it was essential.

I came to understand that **"the biggest risk is not taking one."** Staying in my comfort zone might have felt safe, but it was also holding me back. Leaving the classroom wasn't just about seeking financial stability—it was about breaking free from the limitations I had unknowingly imposed on myself.

The realization that my skills as an educator—problem-solving, communication, empathy— could be repurposed was a turning point. These were the same abilities that had helped me reach struggling students, collaborate with colleagues, and lead as an administrator. They were valuable beyond the boundaries of the classroom, and I began to see how they could thrive in new contexts.

Adopting a growth mindset also meant reframing how I saw my decision to leave education. I wasn't abandoning it; I was evolving. I wasn't walking away from my passion for teaching; I was finding new ways to amplify its impact. Through entrepreneurship, I realized I could create solutions that would support not just my own family but also the students and educators who were still deeply connected to my heart.

Shifting to a growth mindset didn't happen overnight. It required reflection, vulnerability, and a willingness to embrace discomfort. It was about letting go of the fear of failure and focusing instead on the potential for growth. Most importantly, it was about recognizing that I had the power to redefine my own narrative.

If you're feeling stuck or wondering if it's time to make a change, I encourage you to think about the mindset you bring to the table. Are you holding yourself back because of fear or uncertainty? Or are you willing to take the leap, trust your skills, and bet on your ability to grow?

A growth mindset isn't just about believing in the possibility of change—it's about actively pursuing it. It's about realizing that you're not just the sum of where you've been, but the potential of where you can go. For me, that mindset was the key to unlocking the next chapter of my life, and it can be the same for you.

In the next section, we'll dive deeper into how to identify the transferable skills you already have and how to position them for success beyond your current role. Change isn't just possible—it's waiting for you to embrace it.

The Leap from Educator to Embarker: Charlotte Charter and the Separation of Church and State (of Mind)

I met Charlotte Charter during my early years in education. From the very beginning, her approachable demeanor and sharp insights stood out. Though we didn't work together directly, we often crossed paths at professional events and quickly built a strong rapport.

With her background in business and finance, Chalotte had chosen education as her way of making a difference. She was the kind of person who could see opportunity where others only saw obstacles, and her perspective on blending financial acumen with educational vision fascinated me. Over the years, we kept in touch, exchanging ideas about the triumphs and trials of working in education.

When I launched my tutoring company, Charlotte reached out to reconnect. Feeling a mix of pride and curiosity, I invited her to lunch at a local steakhouse—partly to show off my success and partly to hear about her latest endeavors. Over the course of that meal, Charlotte shared something unexpected.

She and her business partner, also a school administrator, were feeling trapped. They were frustrated—professionally and financially. "We're stuck," Charlotte admitted. "We've given so much to education, but it's not giving back to us the way we'd hoped."

I nodded, understanding exactly what she meant. She was describing the same bell that had conditioned so many of us in education: a rigid system that rewarded passion with exhaustion and limited financial growth.

"What are you thinking?" I asked.

Charlotte leaned forward, her voice steady but full of conviction, and explained that she and her partner had been exploring the idea of starting a charter school organization. They didn't have all the details figured out, but one thing was clear—Charlotte had reached her breaking point.

She wasn't just thinking about change; she was ready to *be the* change. She was becoming an "Embarker," stepping into a new journey, even if it felt daunting.

We spent hours talking, with me sharing the lessons I'd learned from building my tutoring company—the pitfalls, the triumphs, and the mistakes I'd made along the way. At one point, she asked, "Was it worth it?"

Without hesitation, I replied, "Charlotte, I will never go back. My worst day out here is better than my best day in there. Not because I don't still love teaching, but because out here, there's no bell telling me when to move, where to go, or how much I'm worth. Trust me. Take the leap. You won't regret it."

Years later, I ran into Charlotte and her partner at a local street festival. They were standing behind a foldable table, handing out brochures. Curious, I walked over, gave her a hug, and asked, 'What's going on? What are you selling?'"

Charlotte grinned. "I'm not selling anything. We're spreading the word about our new charter school."

Charlotte and her partner had done it. They had broken the bell. They had opened a charter school, starting with a leap of faith and a willingness to embrace uncertainty. Their first hurdle? Finding a location.

That's where Charlotte's business sense kicked in. She reached out to a struggling local church and negotiated to rent unused rooms for classrooms. It was a win–win: the church gained much- needed financial support, and Charlotte's school had a home.

The Bell That Rang Loudest: My Leap into Entrepreneurship

Seeing Charlotte's success reminded me of my own leap of faith—the moment a bell rang in my mind so loudly it shook the ground beneath my feet. That bell came in the form of a discovery buried deep in the No Child Left Behind Act (NCLB). It wasn't just any bell—it was the kind that rings like a five-alarm fire, demanding your attention, igniting your curiosity, and forcing you to stop and listen.

At the time, I was working for a world-renowned publishing company. My life was, on paper, everything I had ever dreamed of. I had a steady paycheck, a solid commission structure, a company van, and the freedom to travel throughout the Florida Keys, Miami, and Fort Lauderdale. For many, it would've been the perfect job, and for a moment, I thought it was for me too.

But when I stumbled across a subsection of NCLB during one of my late-night policy dives, that bell wouldn't stop ringing. It wasn't just a sound—it was a call, urgent and insistent, demanding that I read and reread the section promising federal funding for private tutoring services for low-income students in failing schools—Supplemental Educational Services (SES). It was as though the words themselves leapt off the page, daring me to see the opportunity they held.

This wasn't just another piece of policy. This was an open door, a flashing neon "Exit" sign pointing toward a possibility I never imagined. But then came a terrifying question: *Was I ready to make another leap?*

It had only been a year since I'd left the public school sector to join the textbook publishing world. That first leap had required a monumental shift in my mindset, trading the predictable rhythm of a teacher's schedule for the uncertainty of corporate sales. Now, the bell was calling me to leap again—only this time, the stakes were far higher.

To answer the call would mean leaving behind a steady paycheck and the comfort of a prestigious company to start a business from scratch. I had no blueprint, no business plan, no guarantee of success. It would mean risking financial security for my family, venturing into a world I knew little about, and confronting the sobering statistics that most businesses fail within their first few years.

But I couldn't ignore the bell. It was as if everything in my life had been leading up to this moment. I had already bet on myself once, and I was beginning to trust that I could do it again. What if this opportunity was the one that could change everything—not just for me, but for countless students and educators?

With equal parts fear and determination, I took the leap. I quit my job and started what would become The Education Doctor. It was the boldest decision I had ever made in my life. I spent late nights at a small desk in our bedroom, poring over the language of the law, deciphering every word, and imagining what this could become.

The process of building the business was nothing short of daunting. Becoming a certified "Supplemental Education Services" provider required endless paperwork, navigating complex regulations, and answering what felt like a million questions from skeptical stakeholders. There were moments when the fear of failure loomed so large it felt paralyzing. But every step forward deepened my resolve.

I had no way of knowing then that The Education Doctor would grow into one of the largest tutoring companies in Florida, and eventually expand to Texas, Illinois, and New Mexico. I couldn't have imagined that we would serve tens of thousands of students, paying teachers more than double what they earned elsewhere, and transforming lives on a scale I never thought possible.

That bell wasn't just the start of a new chapter—it was the beginning of a legacy. The decision to leap wasn't just about financial success; it was about answering the call to do something greater. It was about using my skills, my vision, and my courage to create something meaningful.

Every time I look back on that moment—the night I heard the bell ring and chose to leap—I'm reminded of the power of faith in yourself. Faith to believe that the skills you've honed in one field can transcend boundaries. Faith to see an opportunity and chase it, even when fear is screaming at you to stop. And faith to trust that your best days are ahead of you, waiting for you to take the leap to find them.

For whom does the bell toll? For every educator feeling stuck in a system that limits their creativity and potential. But what if we stopped answering that bell? What if we broke it?

The leap from educator to entrepreneur isn't easy—it's messy, uncertain, and full of challenges. But with the frameworks I lay out in this book, you'll have the tools to step into something bigger.

Charlotte's success and my own experience are proof of one thing: the growth mindset isn't limited to one field (as you'll read about in the next section) or one dream. It's about recognizing your unique skills, embracing change, and creating something transformative. It's about daring to believe that your best days are ahead of you—and then taking the leap to make them happen.

A Teacher's Journey to Financial Freedom–The Story of Frida Finance

Frida Finance was the kind of teacher every school dreams of having—a dedicated middle school math teacher and PE coach who poured everything she had into her students. In the classroom, she was known for making complex math problems seem simple. On the field, she had a knack for inspiring young athletes to believe in themselves. Her impact was undeniable. But at home? The weight of financial strain was a constant shadow.

Frida was caught in the relentless grip of the first P: **Poor.** No matter how many extra hours she worked—whether it was coaching, tutoring, or summer school—her paycheck barely covered the essentials. Bills piled up. Savings? Nonexistent. The dream of a comfortable life for her family felt like a distant fantasy, and the mounting pressure began to chip away at the joy she once felt for teaching.

As the years passed, that financial stress turned into something deeper: **frustration.** Frida couldn't ignore the nagging sense that the very system she had dedicated her life to wasn't just underpaying her—it was undervaluing her. Passion and purpose didn't translate into financial stability, and the dream of doing meaningful work while securing a better future seemed out of reach. That frustration became the second P: **Pissed-Off.**

One night, after another long day at school and an evening sorting through emails, parent messages, and unfinished assignments, Frida reached her breaking point. "There's got to be more than this," she muttered to herself. Determined to change her circumstances, she dove into researching side hustles— anything that could ease the financial strain.

That's when she stumbled upon an ad for a financial services seminar. It was specifically tailored to public sector employees like teachers, police officers, and first responders. Intrigued but skeptical, Frida decided to check it out.

That seminar changed everything. As she sat at the back of the room, listening to a charismatic speaker break down financial strategies, Frida felt a spark she hadn't felt in years. Suddenly, it clicked: her skills as a teacher—explaining complex concepts and breaking them down into simple, actionable steps—were exactly what people needed to understand financial literacy. Her gift for connecting with people and building trust made her a natural fit for the financial world.

For the first time in years, Frida felt hope. She signed up for the company's training program and dove in headfirst. Nights that used to be spent grading papers were now dedicated to studying retirement planning, insurance, and investment strategies. Her math background gave her a strong foundation, but it was her ability to teach that set her apart. Clients didn't just listen to Frida—they *understood* her. She made intimidating financial topics approachable, empowering people to take control of their futures.

What started as a side hustle soon grew into something much bigger. Within a year, Frida's part- time earnings were outpacing her teaching salary. For the first time, she wasn't just surviving— she was thriving. The decision to leave teaching wasn't an easy one, but Frida knew it was time to embrace the third P: **Proud.** Proud of her growth, proud of the courage it took to bet on herself, and proud of the life she was building for her family.

Frida didn't just trade her teaching career for financial services—she carried her teaching heart with her. She focused on helping fellow educators, first responders, and public sector workers understand their financial options. The same patience and empathy that made her a beloved teacher now made her a trusted financial advisor.

Today, Frida travels the country hosting workshops and seminars, showing educators and public servants that they don't have to feel stuck or undervalued. She's built a thriving business, achieved financial independence, and transformed her life—and the lives of countless others.

Frida's journey from **Poor,** to **Pissed-Off,** to **Proud** has become a blueprint for anyone ready to rewrite their story.

Reflecting on her journey, Frida often says, "Everything I needed to succeed, I learned as a teacher. The ability to listen, to connect, and to make complex ideas simple—those skills didn't just transfer; they *transformed* my new career." Her story is proof that the skills educators hone every day are more valuable than they realize—and that they can unlock opportunities far beyond the walls of a classroom.

Frida didn't just break free from financial insecurity—she built a legacy. By embracing change, learning new skills, and leveraging the talents she already had, Frida redefined what was possible. Her story stands as a reminder to every educator feeling stuck: the leap may be scary, but the rewards of stepping into your potential are worth it.

Unlocking Potential: Educators as Entrepreneurs

For many education professionals, the idea of stepping outside the traditional system feels daunting. After all, the familiar rhythms of the classroom, the district office, or the administrator's seat often come with the comfort of routine—but they also come with limitations. What so many fail to realize is this: the skills you've honed as an educator are not only versatile but incredibly valuable. They have the power to make a significant impact beyond the boundaries of the education system. The key lies in reimagining how those skills can be applied and embracing a growth mindset to unlock new opportunities.

While this book primarily focuses on teachers, it's a resource for *anyone* who works in education or other helping professions and feels stuck, undervalued, or unappreciated. The principles and strategies I share aren't exclusive to the classroom. They are universal for educators— or the "Extended Educator"—whether you're a principal, counselor, speech-language pathologist (SLP), occupational therapist (OT), athletic coach, or even a college professor. If you're ready to reimagine your potential and redefine your professional path, this is your guide.

EXTENDED EDUCATOR

Your Title Isn't Your Ceiling

Whether you're a therapist, athletic coach, or school leader, the call to break the bell is yours too. The title you carry, whether "Dr.," "Coach," or "Principal," doesn't define you. Comfort, fear, or routine, however, can become the ships that keep you anchored.

- **Therapists:** Maybe your "ship" is the clinic. You've built a caseload, you get steady referrals, and starting your own practice feels like a risk. But what if it's not a risk—it's a reward waiting for action? Start small: build a client base, test teletherapy options, research platforms like SimplePractice. Burn that ship one referral at a time.
- **Coaches:** You've built your reputation on the field, court, track, pool, gym, etc. But your leadership, strategy, and teaching mindset extend beyond school sports. Whether it's launching a private coaching program, leading online trainings, or building a youth mentorship brand, your potential impact is bigger than one team.
- **Administrators:** Letting go of your title might be the scariest part (trust me, I know). Principal. Director. Superintendent. But what if those leadership skills became your brand? What if your years of experience became a leadership academy, a podcast, or a consulting firm?

Burning the ships doesn't mean reckless quitting—it means making a plan, setting a date, and taking the first step. When we stop anchoring our ships in safe ports, we start sailing into a vast future.

Extended Educator Reflection:

Are you building the life you dreamed of—or waiting for "someday"?

Therapists and coaches: Take 5 minutes and ask yourself:

- What is one dream you've deferred?
- What fear keeps it from becoming reality?
- What's one small step you can take today?

If not now, when?

Mini-Win:

Small actions have a cumulative effect. Today, it's identifying one skill. Tomorrow, it's acting on an idea sparked by this reflection. Over time, these small wins snowball into meaningful change, creating a clear path toward the life and career you deserve. Transformation is a journey, and every step, no matter how small, moves you closer to your goals.

The question is: *Are you ready to take it?*

Reflection:

List three significant events or moments in your life that have left a lasting impact on you (e.g., challenges, achievements, or transitions).

- Event 1:
- Event 2:
- Event 3:

Why were these moments pivotal?

Next Chapter, New Challenge: Burning the Ships

Embracing a growth mindset is the first step, but real transformation demands action. You've recognized that your skills, passion, and potential extend beyond the classroom or the school office—now comes the moment of decision. Will you hold onto the familiar, or will you commit fully to the next stage of your journey?

Moving from **Educator to Embarker** was about seeing the possibilities. Now, transitioning from **Embarker to Entrepreneur** requires something even greater: the courage to **burn the ships**—to leave behind the safety nets that keep you tethered to what's comfortable and step fully into what's possible.

In the next chapter, we'll explore the pivotal moment when hesitation must give way to commitment. Endings are not failures; they are the fuel for new beginnings. It's time to take the leap, embrace uncertainty, and set a course for a future where you define your own success. Are you ready? Let's go.

CHAPTER 3:

Endings, New Beginnings – Burning the Ships

The moment I decided to step away from my career in education, I felt like I was standing at the edge of a storm—caught between the familiar safety of the shore and the unknown expanse of the open sea. Leaving wasn't just about walking away from a paycheck or retirement benefits. It was about letting go of an identity that had defined me for so long.

I remember vividly the day I sat in the district's HR office, waiting to process my resignation. The officer assisting me looked at me with a mix of confusion and curiosity. "Are you sure you don't want to take a leave of absence instead?" she asked. After all, many former teachers and administrators opted for the safety net of a leave—a chance to try something new while keeping a way back if things didn't work out.

But I knew that wasn't an option for me. If I left that door cracked open, it would become a temptation—a crutch I might lean on the moment things got hard. I couldn't allow myself the luxury of retreat. If I was going to take this leap, I had to be all in.

As I signed the paperwork, I couldn't help but think of Hernán Cortés, the Spanish conquistador who famously ordered his men to burn their ships upon reaching the shores of the New World. By destroying their means of retreat, he forced them to face the challenges ahead with complete commitment. For me, this was no different. I was burning the ships—not out of recklessness, but out of necessity. There could be no turning back.

By destroying their means of retreat, he forced them to face the challenges ahead with complete commitment. For me, this was no different. I was burning the ships, not out of recklessness, but out of necessity. There could be no turning back.

Walking away wasn't just about leaving a job; it was about leaving behind a leadership role where I had invested so much of myself—my energy, my heart, and my belief in what education could accomplish. The weight of the decision was crushing. I thought of my team, my students, and the families who trusted me. Was I letting them down? Would my departure feel like a betrayal of the mission I had dedicated my life to?

It wasn't the first time I had wrestled with such feelings. Years earlier, I had faced a similar internal struggle when I left the classroom to become an administrator. Teaching wasn't just a job—it was my purpose. I knew my students—their stories, their dreams, their struggles. The relationships I built with them were the lifeblood of my career.

When the opportunity to move into administration came, I felt torn. I knew I could make a broader impact—supporting teachers, influencing policies, and creating a better environment for students on a larger scale. But that shift came with a cost: stepping away from the personal, day-to-day connections that had brought me so much fulfillment.

It took months to reconcile that decision, but eventually, I made peace with it by reframing it as an evolution of my purpose. I wasn't leaving teaching—I was expanding my role within it.

Now, years later, the stakes were even higher. This time, I wasn't just stepping away from the classroom or an administrative chair—I was stepping away from education altogether. The guilt came rushing back, magnified by the weight of my responsibilities and the love I had for the mission.

At the same time, I couldn't ignore another truth weighing on me: my family. Despite the long hours, the accolades, and the sacrifices, we were still struggling. My wife and I were raising twin daughters in a cramped townhouse, constantly juggling bills and bracing for the next financial strain. Month after month, the stress was the same, and it became painfully clear that my passion for education wasn't enough to sustain the life we needed.

I had fought so hard to break free from the cycle of poverty, yet here I was, still caught in its grip. The tug-of-war inside me was relentless. On one side was the mission, the people, and the purpose I had dedicated my life to. On the other was my family—their needs, their future, and my growing realization that I couldn't give them what they deserved if I stayed on the same path.

The guilt was crushing, but so was the frustration. I knew that if I stayed, my frustration would eventually turn into resentment, and that would undermine everything I cared about. After many sleepless nights, tears, and honest conversations with my wife, I came to a critical realization: leaving didn't mean abandoning education or the people I cared about. It meant finding a new way to honor my purpose.

Just as I had reconciled leaving the classroom for administration, I began to see this next step as another evolution—not an end, but a new beginning. It was about expanding my impact in a way that allowed me to prioritize my family and my well-being.

And so, with equal parts heartbreak and hope, I burned the ships. I walked away from the steady paycheck, the predictable routine, and the identity I had worn for so long. It wasn't easy. It wasn't without doubt. But it was necessary.

This leap wasn't about giving up—it was about creating space for something bigger. It was about proving that educators could thrive in ways the system never allowed. It was about showing that stepping away doesn't mean leaving behind who you are. It means creating the freedom to embrace who you're meant to become.

That decision was the beginning of a journey that would challenge me, transform me, and ultimately lead to the creation of The Education Doctor, a business that would not only change my life but also the lives of thousands of students and educators across the country.

Burning the ships was the boldest decision I've ever made. It wasn't without fear, but it was full of purpose. And in the end, it wasn't about walking away—it was about stepping into something greater.

The Power of Commitment

Burning the ships isn't about acting recklessly or tossing caution to the wind. It's about making a decision so resolute, so unshakable, that retreat is no longer an option. It's the bold act of removing the safety net, not to tempt fate, but to focus entirely on what lies ahead.

It's the mindset of full commitment—the kind that leaves no room for retreat. Like Cortés and his ships, success often requires us to go all in, trusting that forward is the only direction worth moving.

While historians may debate the accuracy of this tale, the lesson is universal and timeless: *true growth begins when you commit so deeply that the only way forward is through.*

For me, burning the ships meant leaving behind the comfort, stability, and identity I had spent years building as a school administrator to step into a completely unfamiliar world: educational sales. It wasn't just a career change—it was a life shift, one that demanded everything from me. There was no safety net, no leave of absence to fall back on, no Plan B waiting in the wings.

And yet, that lack of a fallback plan didn't terrify me—it fueled me. The urgency of knowing there was no way back pushed me to learn faster, adapt quicker, and work harder than I ever had before. I wasn't just motivated by ambition; I was driven by necessity. The stakes were high— not just for me, but for my family. Failure simply wasn't an option, and that reality sharpened my focus and deepened my commitment.

But burning the ships isn't a philosophy unique to me. It's a principle that has propelled countless others to achieve extraordinary things.

Take Stephanie Sped, for example, a special education teacher who had dedicated her career to students with special needs. For years, she watched as her school district failed to provide the resources her students desperately needed. Frustrated by systemic obstacles, Stephanie decided to take matters into her own hands. She left her district job to start her own school—a bold and terrifying leap.

Stephanie burned her ships by emptying her savings account, calling on every connection she had, and pitching her vision to funders and community leaders. There were countless rejections. At any point, she could have abandoned her dream and returned to the classroom—but because she had removed the option to go back, she had no choice but to keep moving forward.

Her unwavering commitment eventually paid off. Today, her school serves hundreds of students, providing them with the specialized education and resources they deserve. Stephanie's story isn't just a testament to perseverance; it's a reminder that burning the ships creates a kind of clarity and resolve that's hard to achieve when you're still holding on to what's behind you.

Burning the ships isn't just a dramatic gesture—it's a declaration of ownership over your future. It's a decision to fully embrace the challenges ahead, confront your fears, and put every ounce of energy into making your vision a reality.

For me, it became more than just a strategy—it became a way of life. When I walked away from the steady paycheck, the benefits, and the title I had worked so hard to achieve, it wasn't just about taking a risk. It was about betting on myself. It was about believing that my skills, my passion, and my vision were enough to create something extraordinary.

There were no guarantees. There were no safety nets. But there was one thing I knew for certain: I was *all in.*

That kind of commitment isn't easy, and it doesn't come without sacrifice. There were moments when fear and doubt threatened to creep in. But with no ships to return to, I had no choice but to push forward—and that made all the difference.

The Freedom in Commitment

Burning the ships isn't about recklessness; it's about freedom. It's about freeing yourself from the temptation to retreat, the fear of failure, and the "what ifs" that hold so many people back. It's about stepping fully into your potential, knowing that you're willing to do whatever it takes to make your vision a reality.

When you commit to your future with that level of intensity, something shifts. You stop hedging your bets, and you start playing to win. You stop looking back, and you start moving forward with purpose. And most importantly, you begin to see what you're truly capable of.

For me, burning the ships was the turning point that unlocked a future I never could have imagined. It wasn't easy. It wasn't without struggle. But it was worth every ounce of effort.

So, ask yourself: *What ships are holding you back? What safety nets are keeping you anchored to the shore instead of reaching for the horizon?*

Because here's the truth: the moment you burn the ships, you'll discover something extraordinary—your ability to rise to the occasion and create the life you've always imagined.

And that's where the real journey begins.

Breaking the Bell and Burning the Ships

Breaking the bell and burning the ships are deeply connected—they both represent the courage to abandon what's safe and familiar in pursuit of something greater. The bell symbolizes the routines, limitations, and expectations that have kept you tethered, while burning the ships signifies an unshakable commitment to move forward without the option of retreat.

When you eliminate the safety net and let go of what no longer serves you, something powerful happens: your focus sharpens, your determination grows, and you tap into a resilience you didn't even know you had. You stop hedging your bets and start committing fully to the possibilities ahead.

But let's be real—neither act comes without challenges. Burning the ships doesn't guarantee success, and breaking the bell doesn't erase self-doubt. There will be moments when fear creeps in, when setbacks test your resolve, and when you question whether you made the right choice. These moments aren't just inevitable—they're *essential.*

Why? Because those moments of doubt and uncertainty are where growth truly happens. They're where you prove to yourself what you're capable of. It's in these spaces, when retreat isn't an option, that you discover your ability to adapt, overcome, and rise.

Burning the ships and breaking the bell aren't just bold gestures—they're transformative acts that demand your whole heart and your whole self. They're about creating the conditions for real change by leaving behind what's holding you back and stepping boldly into the life you're meant to build.

It's in the midst of setbacks and doubts that growth begins. Burning the ships isn't about avoiding failure; it's about committing to keep going no matter what. It's about transforming fear into fuel and uncertainty into opportunity. Likewise, breaking the bell isn't simply about leaving behind the routines that once defined you—it's about embracing the freedom to define yourself.

That's what makes these two acts so powerful. They push you out of the comfort zone and into the realm of possibility. They force you to confront your fears, adapt, and grow in ways you never could while clinging to what was safe.

The Kelly Clarkson Moment

I'll never forget the day I felt the full weight of my decision. It was my first big sales assignment, and I was driving a company minivan packed to the brim with sample Biology textbooks, heading south to the Florida Keys for an in-person cold call with the Monroe County School Board.

To say I was nervous would be an understatement. I was equal parts excited and terrified. This was it—the moment I had bet everything on. I had walked away from a career I had spent over a decade building, and here I was, racing toward a future that was completely unwritten.

The "what-ifs" swirled in my mind: What if I fail? What if I'm not good at this? What if I made a huge mistake leaving the stability of the life I knew?

And then it happened.

Kelly Clarkson's hit song, "Breakaway" came on the radio1, and the lyrics hit me like a lightning bolt.

It felt like Kelly was sitting right there in the passenger seat, speaking directly to me. I wasn't just hearing a song—I was living it.

As I crossed one of the countless bridges connecting the Florida Keys to the mainland, I rolled down the windows. The salty ocean breeze rushed in, filling the van with the unmistakable scent of freedom. It wasn't just fresh air—it was hope, optimism, and a surge of possibility.

I thought about all those years I had spent inside the four walls of my school office, with the rhythm of the bell marking my every move—when to teach, when to eat, when to go home. That routine, while predictable, had also kept me confined. But now, the bell was broken.

Kelly's voice soared through the speakers describing her journey from darkness to light. I smiled because that was it. That was exactly what I had done. I had stepped out of the darkness of predictability and limitation, and into the light of possibility and growth.

For the first time, I felt the weight of my decision lift. Sure, fear and self-doubt were still there, riding along like unwelcome passengers. But they were quieter now, overshadowed by something far stronger: an unshakable confidence that I was on the right path.

The road ahead wasn't just taking me to the Monroe County School Board for a cold call, it was leading me to a better life for my family—a life where I could provide for my wife and twin daughters in ways I never could before. In that moment, with the breeze in my face and a van full of Biology textbooks in the back, I realized something profound: I wasn't just selling books - I was rewriting my story.

I had burned my ships, and there was no turning back.

My future wasn't tied to a bell, a classroom, or a school district anymore. It wasn't in the comfort of what I had known but rather somewhere out there, on the open road, waiting for me to embrace it.

The Bird in the Cage with an Open Door

That drive over the ocean reminded me of something I'd seen years before: a bird perched contentedly inside an open cage.

As a little boy, I would often accompany my grandmother on visits to her friends' homes. These outings were usually uneventful to me—conversations between adults that didn't hold my attention, the occasional cookie offered to keep me quiet, and familiar settings that quickly faded from memory. But one visit stood out.

I remember sitting in a kitchen with my grandmother and one of her friends when I noticed something that both confused and fascinated me. Hanging by the kitchen window was a small birdcage and inside was a tiny bird—a parakeet, I believe. At first, there was nothing particularly extraordinary about it. But then I noticed something unusual: the cage door was wide open.

I couldn't understand it. The bird wasn't locked inside. It was free to leave. And yet, it stayed perched inside the cage, just a few feet away from the open window. Outside, other birds flew freely, chirping and calling to one another as they darted across the sky. Surely this little bird could hear them, sense the freedom just beyond the window. Yet, it didn't move. It stayed in the cage, waiting—content, it seemed, to remain in the safety of its small, enclosed world.

I remember feeling both curious and anxious about it. What if the bird suddenly flew out the window? What if it got lost or hurt? I wanted to ask my grandmother's friend why she kept the door open, but something about the moment made me keep quiet.

At the time, I didn't understand why this image stayed with me. It was one of those memories that lodged itself in my mind without explanation, something I'd revisit years later with a new perspective.

Now, as I reflect on that scene, I see it as a metaphor for the struggle so many of us face when deciding whether to step out of the familiar and into the unknown.

"Bird in an Open Cage" by Alyssa M. Ferrer

That image stuck with me because it's such a clear metaphor for the choices we make. The cage represents the routines, fears, and doubts that keep us confined. The open door is the opportunity for freedom, but stepping through it requires courage, trust, and the willingness to embrace uncertainty.

The bird's hesitation reflects a universal truth about nature: we grow accustomed to the predictability of our routines, even when they limit us. The safety of the known feels easier than the risk of stepping into the unknown. We tell ourselves it's better to stay where it's familiar and safe than to risk failure or disappointment by flying into something new.

But the reality is this: **the cage is a choice.**

The bird in the cage chooses to stay, just as we often choose to remain within the boundaries of our own fears, doubts, and routines. The door is open, the possibility of freedom is right there, but stepping outside requires us to confront what's holding us back. It's not just a fear of failure— it's fear of what success might demand of us. It's the fear of losing the comfort of what we've always known, even if that comfort comes with limitations.

As I drove over that bridge to my first sales assignment, with Kelly Clarkson's "Breakaway" still echoing in my ears, I realized that the cage wasn't just a metaphor—it was my life. For years, I had lived inside the cage of predictability. The consistent rhythm of the bell, the steady paycheck, the title on my business card—they were all part of that cage. And while it felt secure, it wasn't what I truly wanted.

Now, with the open road stretching out in front of me and the ocean breeze rushing through the van, I understood that I had made my choice. I had stepped through the open door, leaving the cage behind. It wasn't easy, and it wasn't without fear. But for the first time, I felt what it was like to fly.

The bird in the cage may see the open door and hesitate, but it's only when it takes flight that it truly discovers what it's capable of. The same is true for all of us. Freedom isn't just about escaping the cage—it's about trusting ourselves to navigate the unknown and embracing the possibilities that come with it.

Because the truth is, the cage may feel safe, but it's never where we're meant to stay.

Stepping out of the cage—breaking the bell, burning the ships, taking the leap—doesn't guarantee an easy path. There will be turbulence, uncertainty, and moments of doubt. But those are the moments when growth happens. They're the moments when you discover your strength, your resilience, and your ability to soar.

That little bird by the kitchen window may have been content to stay on its perch, but I knew I couldn't live that way. I had to fly!

As I crossed that bridge, it hit me—the open sky ahead wasn't just a nice metaphor. It was my future, wide open and ready for me to step into it and make it mine.

From the Bird to the Bird Man

We love to romanticize the idea of breaking free. But no one talks about how terrifying freedom can actually feel.

There's a popular movie that follows the lives of men inside a brutal prison. One of its characters is known for caring for a bird within his prison cell—feeding it, nurturing it, finding meaning and comfort in its presence. He became a caretaker of life in a place built for confinement.

But when he's finally released after decades behind bars, he doesn't celebrate. He crumbles because the world outside feels foreign. The walls that once symbolized punishment had become comfort. In essence, after a lifetime inside, the prison doesn't feel like punishment anymore - it feels like protection and identity.

And when that's taken away—even if it's in the name of freedom—it doesn't always feel like a gift. To the Bird Man his freedom felt like grief and loss. That moment has always stuck with me because that's what systems do. That's what school buildings can do. They convince us that the safety, known, structured path of our teaching career is the only one worth following. The bell rings, the day begins. You show up, give your all, and do it again tomorrow. Repeat, and repeat.

But what happens when that ringing starts to feel more like a cage than a calling?

What happens when that inner voice won't stay quiet—consistently whispering, *"There's something else out there for you"*?

That's the tension I want to sit in with you—because I've lived it.

Breaking the Bell isn't just about walking away from something, it's about walking toward something more, even when your knees are shaking. And if you've ever felt stuck between the security of what you know and the risk of what could be… just know, you're not alone.

So, the question is this: *Are you the bird waiting for the next predictable meal, content with the security of the cage? Or are you ready to take the leap and discover what lies beyond the open door?*

Preparing to Burn the Ships

Building a Financial Runway

Burning the ships isn't about reckless abandon—it's about strategic commitment. You don't burn the ships while you're still at sea, drifting in uncertainty. That would be reckless. Instead, you burn the ships when you've reached solid ground, scoped out the landscape, and made a calculated decision to move forward. Preparation is key, and it's what allows you to commit fully to your vision when the time is right.

When I prepared to burn my ships, I worked tirelessly, essentially holding down two full-time jobs. By day, I represented the textbook publisher, giving my all to a role I knew would soon be in my rearview mirror. But by night, I was laying the groundwork for my future.

Every evening, I sat at my desk, often working until the early hours of the morning, building the foundation for the tutoring business that would eventually become my livelihood. It was grueling, exhausting, and overwhelming at times, but I knew exactly why I was doing it.

Every ounce of energy I was putting into those late nights was going toward *my company, not someone* else's. That knowledge fueled me. While the finances weren't guaranteed, I believed in the work I was doing and the vision I was building. By the time I was ready to burn the ships, I had created enough of a runway to step forward with confidence.

Burning the ships doesn't mean acting impulsively. It means committing to your future with the conviction that you're ready to move forward. It's about ensuring that your energy is focused on building your own dream—not staying tethered to someone else's.

Action Steps

If you're preparing for your own leap, think about how you can start building your runway now. Assess what groundwork you can lay while still in your current role. This might mean dedicating evenings or weekends to crafting your plan, learning new skills, or exploring opportunities that align with your vision.

It's not easy to juggle multiple responsibilities, but every step you take now is an investment in your future. When the time comes to make your move, you'll know you're not burning the ships recklessly—you're burning them because you've already set yourself up to succeed.

Identify Transferable Skills:

As educators, we often underestimate how broad and valuable our skills are. The truth is, the abilities you've honed—communication, leadership, problem-solving, and adaptability—are highly transferable to other industries.

I began my transition by mapping out the skills I had cultivated over the years. My ability to communicate complex ideas in simple, actionable ways became a strength in client relations and sales. Managing a classroom taught me leadership and organizational skills that prepared me for leading teams in business. Years of navigating classroom challenges made me an effective problem-solver in entrepreneurial situations.

I also discovered that traits like empathy, adaptability, and organization—second nature to educators—were highly valued in fields like corporate training, consulting, and customer service. These insights not only boosted my confidence but also helped me articulate the value I could bring to new industries.

Make a list of your transferable skills. Be specific. Think about how lesson planning could translate to project management or how mentoring students might apply to coaching professionals. Once you've mapped your skills, research industries or roles that interest you. Look for overlaps between your experience and what's in demand. To go even further, connect with professionals in those industries to gain insight into how your background can add value.

Leverage Your Network:

One of the most powerful tools in any career transition is your network. The relationships you've built throughout your career—colleagues, mentors, former students, and professional connections—can offer invaluable guidance and open doors you didn't know existed.

During my journey, I reached out to people whose careers intrigued me. I asked for advice, learned about their paths, and explored how my skills might translate into their industries. These conversations were eye-opening. A former colleague who had transitioned into educational sales became an important mentor, helping me see how I could leverage my skills in a completely new space. Their guidance gave me clarity and confidence as I took my first steps into sales.

Expanding my network was just as critical. I participated in industry-specific events to connect with people outside of my immediate circle. Networking wasn't just about finding business leads—it was about learning from others' experiences and understanding how to navigate a new field.

Start mapping out your network. Identify people in your circle who have pursued paths that interest you and reach out to them. Ask about their journey and what advice they might have for someone considering a similar leap. Beyond your current connections, focus on growing your network. Join relevant groups, attend webinars or conferences, and connect with people in your desired field. Every conversation is an opportunity to gain insight, build relationships, and expand your horizons.

EXTENDED EDUCATOR

You Can't Take the Old Boat to a New Shore

Here's the truth most people won't say out loud in leadership meetings: staying stuck is safer than starting over.

For many of us—especially those with big titles or specialized licenses—the real ship we have to burn is identity. You're the AP everyone goes to during a fight. You're the OT parents count on to help work the chaos into calm. You're the coach who builds discipline like clockwork. You're proud of that, and you should be.

But if that role becomes your entire anchor, you'll miss the chance to grow into something even greater.

Burning the ships doesn't mean burning bridges. It means no longer building your life around fear. Canceling that backup plan. Saying no to a "safe" job offer that keeps you small. Choosing the fire of becoming over the comfort of being known.

Your next chapter isn't going to hand you confidence—it's going to demand courage.

Mini-Win:

Identify one "ship" you'll burn this week—a habit, mindset, or obligation holding you back. Take the first concrete step to let it go, then share your commitment with an accountability partner.

The Burn-the-Ships Commitment Plan

Step	Example Action
Identify Your Ships	Write down fears or safety nets keeping you stuck.
Create a Plan	Side hustles, moonlighting, learning a new skill, or networking.
Commit Fully	Set a bold deadline or announce your decision publicly.

Burning the ships isn't about recklessness—it's about intentionality. By preparing thoughtfully, you create a bridge between fear and confidence, ensuring that your leap is supported by a solid foundation. Whether it's building a financial runway, identifying your transferable skills, or leveraging your network, each step you take is a step toward freedom and growth.

Your Bridge to Confidence

Action Steps: Taking bold action starts with clarity and commitment. These actionable steps will help you define what's holding you back, prepare for your transition, and take the leap toward your new future.

1. **Define Your Ships**
   Write down one habit, fear, or excuse that's keeping you from moving forward. Be honest with yourself—recognizing these barriers is the first step to overcoming them.

Example: Fear of financial instability → Build a six-month emergency fund.

2. **Create Your Exit Plan**
   List three steps you'll take before commiting to your new career. These steps will help you gain confidence and prepare for the transition. Example: Gain a certification, secure a mentor, or research your new industry.

3. **Set a Date**
   Choose a realistic but challenging timeline for your transition. Setting a date creates accountability and gives you a clear target to work toward.

Next Chapter, New Challenge: If Not Now, When?

Burning the ships is about committing fully to your vision—choosing to act on your dreams now, not waiting for the elusive *someday. In this chapter, we'll explore how embracing the future starts* with breaking free of the belief that there's always more time. Because the truth is, time is the one resource we can never get back.

PART 2:

Answering the Bell: The Call for Change

CHAPTER 4:

Embrace the Future – If Not Now, When?

Mrs. Russell's Dream Cabin

Mrs. Russell was unlike anyone I had ever met. She was an eclectic soul with a heart of gold and an office that felt more like a metaphysical shop than a school counselor's workspace. On my first day as a school administrator, she breezed into my office carrying a smoldering bundle of sage, ready to cleanse the space before I moved in.

I stood there, caught between confusion and amusement, holding the few boxes that represented my career—certificates, two Teacher of the Year awards, and my doctorate degree, ready to adorn the drab gray brick walls.

At first glance, I never imagined we'd become friends. Mrs. Russell, who was old enough to be my mother, often wore wolf t-shirts, flowing skirts, and necklaces made of beads and crystals. Her calm, grounded presence seemed worlds apart from my driven, ambitious mindset. But over time, we found common ground. Sharing lunches in the teachers' lounge turned into trading stories about our lives and talking about our dreams.

At that point in my career, I was laser-focused on climbing the ladder, ambitiously working toward the superintendency (spoiler alert: I never got there). Mrs. Russell, on the other hand, was counting down the days to retirement. Her dream was simple, yet profound: to finish building her log cabin in the mountains of North Carolina.

Over the next two years, I watched her excitement grow as she shared pictures of the cabin's progress during our lunches. Each milestone—from the foundation being poured to the walls going up—was a testament to her determination. She happily shared stories of contractors who were late or over budget, but her eyes always sparkled with hope. That cabin wasn't just a house; it was her sanctuary, the culmination of years of hard work and sacrifice.

Every other weekend, she commuted from South Florida to North Carolina to oversee the construction. At first, I couldn't understand why she hadn't already retired. She had earned it.

But the more we talked, the clearer it became: she was working those extra years to ensure her dream was fully realized.

When her retirement day finally arrived, we celebrated with a small party in the teachers' lounge. It wasn't the grand send-off she deserved, but Mrs. Russell didn't seem to care. Her joy wasn't tied to the party—it was tied to the life waiting for her in the mountains.

For a few weeks after her retirement, we kept in touch. She sent me photos of herself on her cabin's porch, surrounded by trees and wildlife, soaking in the peace she had worked so hard to create. She described watching deer wander through her yard, the cool mountain breeze on her face, and the feeling of finally being home.

And then, just a few months later, I got the news: Mrs. Russell had passed away.

Her death shook me to my core. I couldn't stop asking myself: *Was it worth it?* All those years of sacrifice, commuting, and waiting for "someday," only to have so little time to enjoy it?

Her story haunted me. It forced me to look at my own life and ask some hard questions: *Am I on the same path? Am I working tirelessly toward a future that I might never fully get to experience? Is there a better way to live my dreams now?*

Mrs. Russell's story stayed with me. When I finally broke the bell and left the education system to pursue a new path in educational sales, it was her memory that gave me the courage to take the leap. She reminded me that the clock is always ticking, that dreams don't wait, and that "someday" isn't guaranteed.

Your Call to Action: Don't Wait

To all the Mrs. Russell's out there—those who have dreams waiting patiently in the background—this is your reminder: *Don't* wait. Don't let fear, routine, or the safety of the bell hold you back. The dreams you've kept on the back burner are worth pursuing now.

Mrs. Russell's legacy wasn't just her cabin; it was the lesson she left behind: the time to act is today. So take the leap, burn the ships, and embrace the future you've been imagining.

Because **if not now, when?**

The Trap of "Someday"

How often do we catch ourselves saying, "I'll go after my dreams later," or, "I'll make a change when the timing is right"? It's such a common refrain, but the reality is harsh: *"Someday" rarely ever comes.* Waiting for the "perfect time" or "someday" is one of the most dangerous traps we fall into.

The truth is, life will never feel perfectly aligned for big decisions. There will always be uncertainties, risks, and reasons to delay. The to-do lists will never end, the finances might not feel just right, and fear of the unknown will never completely disappear. But the biggest risk isn't failing—it's waiting so long that your dreams fade into distant memories.

Think about the dreams you've been putting off. How long have you been telling yourself you'll get to them *eventually?* How often have you let fear or "the right timing" hold you back?

Here's the truth that Mrs. Russell's story taught me: *the clock is always ticking.* You can't control how much time you have, but you can control how you spend it. Acting on your dreams today, even in small ways, is the only way to ensure they don't stay stuck in the realm of "someday."

EXTENDED EDUCATOR

Your Growth Plan Starts Here

Growth isn't about ditching your identity and becoming someone new—it's about activating more of who you already are.

Whether you're a:

- **School leader** refining your consulting skills,
- **Counselor** expanding into teletherapy,
- **Coach** building a training curriculum, or
- **SLP/OT/PT** exploring adaptive tech…

Growth begins by identifying your next chapter and applying the skills you have honed over the years.

Action Plan:

1. **Name the gap.** Time management? Financial literacy? Tech tools?
2. **Pick one area to level up.** Keep it simple - just one and focus on it.
3. **Take one step.** Enroll in a course, reach out to a mentor, schedule 30 minutes this week to plan.

Write it down and make it real because progress loves a plan.

Mini-Win:

Identify one small action you can take this week to move closer to your deferred dream. Write it down and commit to completing it.

Time-to-Action Planner

Step	Action Example
Define Your Dream	Write down what you truly want to achieve.
Identify Barriers	List fears or excuses preventing you from acting.
Take One Small Step	Commit to one action today, like networking or research.

Lessons from the Journey

Taking action doesn't mean ignoring obstacles; it means working through them one step at a time. You don't have to leap all at once, but you do have to start.

Action Steps:

1. Write down one dream you've deferred and why.
2. Identify three steps you can take today to move closer to that dream.
3. Take one of those steps before the week ends.

Next Chapter, New Challenge: The Three Personas

Once you've committed to acting on your dreams, the next step is to evaluate your current position. In Chapter 5, we'll help you identify where you are on your journey—from Educator to Embarker to Entrepreneur—and how to take the next step forward. Understanding your current persona is like finding your location on a map: it's essential for charting the path ahead.

CHAPTER 5:
The Three Personas—Educator, Embarker, Entrepreneur

When we step into the classroom for the first time, it's often with a spark—a passion to make a difference, to change lives, to ignite learning. That spark fuels us through the early years, giving us energy and purpose. The joy of seeing a struggling student grasp a concept or the pride in helping a class achieve a milestone becomes the currency that sustains us.

But as the years pass, the repetitive chime of the school bell, the weight of systemic challenges, and the monotony of routine can start to dull that passion. The overwhelming demands, from standardized testing to ever-growing class sizes, begin to chip away at the idealism that brought so many of us into the profession in the first place.

For many educators, this leads to an inevitable question: **Is this all there is?**

That question is not a sign of failure or weakness. In fact, it's the first step toward transformation. It's the whisper of something greater calling you—a realization that the skills, empathy, and leadership you've cultivated in the classroom might have a larger purpose beyond its walls.

Through my journey—and the journeys of countless others—I've learned that breaking free begins with understanding where you are. Over the years, I've identified three distinct personas that define the educator's transformation journey. These personas are not rigid categories but fluid stages, each representing a mindset and a moment of decision. Understanding where you stand is the first step toward moving forward.

The Three Personas

Persona 1: The Educator—Rooted in Purpose

The Educator is the foundation. This is where you begin. In this stage, your identity is tied closely to your classroom, your students, and the school community. You are a master of lesson plans, differentiation strategies, and student engagement. The educator stage is where most of us feel a deep sense of belonging and purpose, at least initially.

But the Educator stage can also become a trap. The longer you stay, the more the routines and limitations of the role can feel like a comfort zone—safe but stifling. If you've ever found yourself daydreaming about a different life but dismissing it because of fear or self-doubt, you're still firmly in the Educator stage.

If you're in this stage, ask yourself: *Am I still fulfilled, or am I starting to feel confined by the bell?*

Persona 2: The Embarker—Exploring New Horizons

The Embarker is the one who dares to step out of the comfort zone. This persona emerges the moment you say, "What if?" It's the first step toward exploring what's possible beyond the school walls.

Embarkers are curious, but they're also cautious. They dip their toes into new opportunities— maybe starting a side hustle, pursuing additional certifications, or attending networking events in unfamiliar industries. This stage is about experimentation and discovery.

It's not always an easy transition. The Embarker faces uncertainty, self-doubt, and even guilt. After all, the identity of being "just a teacher" has been so deeply ingrained that moving beyond it can feel like betrayal. But it's also the stage where possibility starts to replace fear.

This stage can be both exciting and intimidating, filled with questions like: *Can I really do this? What if I fail? Is it worth the risk?*

If you're an Embarker, embrace the uncertainty. This stage is about discovery and growth— allow yourself the space to explore without needing all the answers.

Persona 3: The Entrepreneur–Owning Your Path

The Entrepreneur persona emerges when you've decided to fully commit to a new direction. It's the stage of action, resilience, and self-determination.

As an Entrepreneur, you've burned the ships and stepped boldly into the unknown. You've reframed your skills, built a plan, and are actively creating a life that aligns with your goals and values. This stage isn't without challenges—there will be failures, lessons, and moments of doubt—but it's also where freedom, creativity, and fulfillment thrive.

Entrepreneurs often describe this stage as liberating. For the first time, the bell is gone. There's no schedule dictating when to move, no system confining your growth, and no limits to your potential.

If you're an Entrepreneur, your focus is on building, adapting, and thriving. You've taken control of your story and are writing the chapters on your own terms.

How to Identify Your Persona

As you read through this chapter, reflect on where you see yourself. Are you feeling stuck but unsure of what's next? You're likely in the Educator stage. Are you testing the waters, trying to find what fits? That's the Embarker in you. Or have you already committed to building something new and taking full control of your career? Congratulations—you're stepping into the Entrepreneur persona.

This chapter isn't about judgment or rushing the process. It's about clarity. Each stage has value, and each step is necessary. Recognizing where you are will help you move forward with purpose and confidence.

Let's dive deeper into these personas and uncover the strategies, tools, and mindset shifts that will guide you to the next step in your journey. You've already made the hardest decision: to dream bigger. Now it's time to act.

The Transition: Educator to Embarker to Entrepreneur

Educator: Committed but Constrained

Meet Tracy Tutor. For 15 years, she poured her heart into teaching high school English. Her passion for literature was contagious, and she had a gift for helping students discover their voices through writing. Parents sang her praises, and former students regularly returned to thank her for the profound impact she'd had on their lives.

But beneath the accolades, Tracy felt a growing sense of frustration. Her evenings were spent buried under stacks of essays, weekends consumed by lesson planning, and summers devoted to professional development—yet her paycheck barely covered her rising expenses.

The emotional toll of constantly giving to others without adequate support began to weigh on her.

When Tracy's aging mother needed full-time care, the cracks in her financial and emotional foundation deepened. She felt stuck, asking herself: "Is this all there is? How can I continue making a difference and still support my family?"

Tracy's story is one shared by countless educators. The pressures of the profession—while fulfilling in some ways—often create a sense of being overworked and underappreciated. For Tracy, the realization that something had to change came slowly, through quiet moments of reflection and the mounting urgency of her personal responsibilities.

Embarker: Exploring New Paths

Tracy's story didn't end in frustration. After months of soul-searching and late-night brainstorming, she decided to explore paths outside the classroom. She joined a local writing group, began offering one-on-one tutoring sessions, and attended webinars on freelancing and curriculum development. With each step, she uncovered opportunities she had never considered.

As Tracy began to reimagine her skills and how they could be applied beyond the classroom, she transitioned into the role of an Embarker—someone taking tentative but meaningful steps toward a new chapter.

Charlotte Charter, another Embarker, faced a similar crossroads. After 20 years as a high school principal, Charlotte had a vision for creating a charter school that would better serve students and communities. Yet the thought of leaving her secure position terrified her.

Over lunch one day, Charlotte confessed her fears to me: *"What if I try and fail? What if the funding doesn't come through, or I can't balance the budget? It feels like too much to handle."*

Like Tracy, Charlotte was beginning to see the possibilities, but the uncertainty of stepping into the unknown kept her tethered to the familiar.

Entrepreneur: Thriving in New Territory

Both Tracy and Charlotte eventually took the leap into entrepreneurship, moving beyond their doubts and stepping fully into their new futures.

For Tracy, this meant transforming her love of writing into a successful business as a college essay coach. She now helps students craft compelling applications, drawing on her years of experience teaching writing. Her work is flexible, impactful, and financially rewarding.

Charlotte's path was equally transformative. With a mix of grit and determination, she founded her first charter school. The early days were far from easy—she wrestled with securing funding, hiring staff who shared her vision, and navigating layers of red tape. There were moments of doubt, but her unwavering belief in her mission kept her moving forward.

That perseverance paid off. Charlotte's first school thrived, earning a reputation for its innovative curriculum and student-centered approach. What began as a single school serving a few hundred students soon grew into a network of over two dozen charter schools, each one built on the principles of equity and opportunity.

Your Next Steps

The transition from Educator to Embarker to Entrepreneur is not a straight line; it's a journey of reflection, risk, and reinvention. Whether you see yourself in Tracy's early frustrations or Charlotte's cautious optimism, know that every step forward is an act of courage.

The skills and passion that brought you to education can be the same tools that guide you into a new chapter—one where your impact grows beyond the walls of a classroom, and your potential is fully realized.

As we continue in this chapter, we'll explore practical strategies for making the leap, overcoming fear, and building a future that aligns with your vision. Just like Tracy and Charlotte, your next chapter starts with a single decision to say yes to what's possible.

A Life Transformed

Today, Charlotte's schools serve thousands of students, providing high-quality education to communities that had long been underserved. But the impact of her journey didn't stop with education—it transformed her personal life, too.

Charlotte's success has allowed her to achieve financial freedom, providing the life she always dreamed of for herself and her family. Free from the financial constraints that once burdened her, she now has the time and resources to focus on what matters most: traveling with her loved ones, pursuing her passions, and continuing to grow her legacy. She's a living testament to how stepping out of your comfort zone and embracing risk can lead to rewards far greater than you ever imagined.

Similarly, Tracy has found fulfillment beyond what she once thought possible. No longer confined by the bell, she works on her own schedule, doing work she loves while earning a sustainable income that supports her family. With flexibility and autonomy, she's able to care for her aging mother while also building a thriving coaching business. Her days are filled with meaningful work, but they're also balanced with time for self-care, creativity, and joy.

Both Charlotte and Tracy are proof that the leap from Educator to Embarker to Entrepreneur isn't just about career transformation—it's about life transformation. It's about trading burnout for balance, stagnation for growth, and doubt for confidence.

Your Transformation Awaits

This journey isn't just for people like Charlotte and Tracy—it's for anyone who dares to dream bigger. It's for the teacher grading papers late into the night, wondering if their hard work will ever be truly valued. It's for the administrator who feels stuck in bureaucracy, yearning for a chance to create something meaningful. It's for the educator with a side hustle they're too afraid to pursue full time.

Your transformation begins the moment you recognize that your skills, passion, and experiences are assets, not limitations. The classroom was your training ground—it taught you how to solve problems, inspire others, and adapt to challenges. Now, it's time to take those lessons and apply them in new ways.

As you continue reading, you'll discover actionable strategies for navigating this transition. From identifying your strengths to overcoming fear and building a sustainable business model, this chapter will give you the tools to take the next step forward.

The path from Educator to Embarker to Entrepreneur isn't easy, but it is worth it. And as Charlotte and Tracy's stories show, the rewards—both personal and professional—are more fulfilling than you can imagine.

The road may be challenging, but the journey is worth it. ***If not now, when?***

The Persona Progression

Persona	Mindset	Primary Question
Educator	Passionate but feeling undervalued, financially constrained, or burned out.	"Is this all there is?"
Embarker	Exploring new opportunities, often unsure and hesitant but hopeful.	"What's next?"
Entrepreneur	Confidently building something new, focused on growth and impact.	"How can I expand this?"

The Struggles Behind the Transformation–Case Studies Tracy's Leap

Tracy's leap into entrepreneurship wasn't without its challenges. For months, she wrestled with imposter syndrome.

"Who am I to run a business?" she would think, despite her years of proven success in the classroom. The idea of presenting herself as a professional beyond the label of "teacher" felt daunting. She doubted whether her skills were transferable and whether people would take her seriously.

The first time she pitched her writing-coach services to a parent, her voice shook, and her palms were clammy. She stumbled through her pricing and second-guessed every word she said. But to her surprise, the parent enthusiastically agreed, praising her expertise. Not only that, they referred three friends within weeks.

That moment was a turning point for Tracy—it showed her that her skills were valuable and needed. The years she had spent teaching writing, giving feedback, and coaching students on their essays were exactly what parents and students wanted.

Facing Financial Uncertainty

The unpredictable income was another hurdle. There were weeks when Tracy questioned whether she'd made the right decision to leave her stable teaching job. Bills didn't stop coming, and she had to get creative with her budgeting. She learned to cut unnecessary expenses, leverage free tools to market her business, and prioritize financial planning.

But Tracy adapted. She celebrated even the smallest wins—a new client, a glowing testimonial, a milestone in her monthly revenue. Over time, she discovered patterns in her business and built systems that helped her manage her workload and forecast her income.

Persistence Pays Off

Tracy's persistence paid off. As word spread about her coaching services, her business grew. Parents raved about her ability to help students not only improve their essays but also develop confidence in their storytelling.

Today, Tracy makes double her teaching salary, works fewer hours, and has the flexibility to care for her mother. She spends her mornings working with clients and her afternoons pursuing her own creative writing projects. She no longer dreads Sunday nights or feels the crushing weight of endless grading. What once felt like an impossible dream is now her reality.

Tracy reflects on her journey with a sense of pride and gratitude. "It wasn't easy," she admits, "but stepping out of my comfort zone was the best decision I ever made. I'm finally living the life I used to dream about."

The Truth About Transformation

Tracy's story reveals an essential truth about transformation: it's messy, uncomfortable, and often riddled with doubt. But it's also where growth happens. The struggles she faced—imposter syndrome, financial uncertainty, and fear of failure—are universal. Every Embarker and Entrepreneur encounters them.

The difference between those who stay stuck and those who succeed is perseverance. Tracy didn't let her fears stop her. She pushed through them, learned from her mistakes, and kept moving forward, one small step at a time.

Your journey will have its own challenges. You'll doubt yourself, face setbacks, and feel tempted to retreat into the safety of the familiar. But remember this: **every struggle is part of the process.**

Steve's Leap

Steve Supe was no stranger to the pressures and politics of education. After a distinguished career as a teacher, school administrator, district leader, and superintendent across multiple school districts, Steve had built a reputation as a no-nonsense advocate for students. He was a leader who bucked the norm to fight for the equal treatment of all students, earning respect from peers and even critics.

Steve was also a familiar face on the education conference circuit. From delivering riveting keynotes to leading transformative workshops, his presence was magnetic. But behind the scenes, Steve began noticing cracks in the conference model he had come to know so well.

The same old sessions. The same old vendors. The same lack of meaningful innovation.

"Why are we doing this the same way we've done it for decades?" he would ask himself. Conferences had become a box to check, rather than a source of inspiration or actionable insights. Steve believed that educators—especially those in leadership roles—deserved better.

That's when he heard his bell ringing for change.

A Bold Vision for Change

Steve didn't just complain about the problem; he set out to fix it. He gathered a small group of trusted superintendents—leaders who shared his passion for progress and his willingness to challenge outdated norms. Together, they began brainstorming a new model for professional gatherings.

What emerged was a bold vision: *a conference for educators, by educators.*

This wasn't just about shaking things up. Steve wanted to create a space where superintendents, aspiring district leaders, and other key decision-makers could come together to share authentic experiences, exchange practical solutions, and connect in meaningful ways. He also envisioned a collaborative environment where vendors and district leaders could build real partnerships, moving beyond transactional relationships.

Their first event was modest in scale but monumental in impact. Attendees praised the conference's authenticity, relevance, and energy. Vendors valued the opportunity to engage directly with decision-makers, forging connections that felt personal and mutually beneficial.

The Struggles of Reinvention

Steve's leap into entrepreneurship wasn't without its hurdles.

Starting from scratch meant navigating a steep learning curve—everything from event planning logistics to marketing strategies had to be learned on the fly. And while Steve's reputation helped draw initial interest, he still faced skepticism from those accustomed to the traditional conference model.

"Who's going to take us seriously?" Steve worried aloud during the early days. "We're just a handful of superintendents trying to shake up a multi-billion-dollar industry."

Finances were another challenge. Securing venues, hiring staff, and managing technology platforms required a significant upfront investment, and for a while, Steve worried he had bitten off more than he could chew.

But what kept Steve going was his unshakeable belief in his mission. Every time an attendee approached him to say, "This was the most valuable conference I've ever attended," or a vendor expressed gratitude for the genuine connections they had made, Steve's doubts were replaced by resolve.

A Legacy of Impact

Today, Steve's conferences are some of the most well-attended and sought-after events in the education industry. What started as a small gathering has grown into a movement, drawing thousands of educators, aspiring leaders, and school vendors from across the country.

For Steve, the success isn't just financial—though he has built a thriving business that has created new revenue streams for himself and his team. The real reward lies in the impact his conferences have had on the education landscape.

He's created a platform where educators can come together to solve real problems, share groundbreaking ideas, and build relationships that drive change.

And for vendors, Steve's model has redefined what collaboration looks like, creating a win–win dynamic that benefits everyone involved.

A Life Transformed

Steve's journey into entrepreneurship has transformed his personal life as well. Free from the demands and politics of district leadership, he now has the time and freedom to focus on what truly matters to him. He travels with his family, mentors the next generation of educational leaders, and continues to refine and expand his conferences.

Steve's story is a testament to what's possible when you pair experience with vision and courage. By stepping out of his comfort zone and reimagining what education conferences could be, he not only changed his own life but also the lives of thousands of educators and leaders.

Your Transformation Awaits

Steve's leap, like Tracy's, is proof that transformation isn't reserved for the boldest or the most fearless—it's for anyone willing to take the first step. It starts with seeing the cracks in the system and believing that you can do better.

As you continue reading, ask yourself:

- What needs fixing in your world?
- What would it look like if you were the one to create the solution?

Your journey may not be easy, but just like Steve and Tracy, you'll discover that the rewards— both personal and professional—are worth every challenge along the way. Let's keep building.

Educators:

Reflect on what excites you most about teaching. Is it the way you ignite curiosity in your students? The creativity in designing lessons? The relationships you build? Consider how these passions could evolve into a new career path, such as coaching, writing, or consulting. Write down one specific area of teaching you love and imagine how it could be applied outside the classroom.

Embarkers:

Focus on gaining new skills or certifications that support your transition. Consider taking a short online course in business fundamentals, marketing, or project management. Look for side gigs or freelance opportunities that let you test new waters without giving up the safety of your current role. Write down one skill you want to develop or one side project you'd like to try.

Entrepreneurs:

Now that you've taken the leap, explore ways to scale your impact. Could you partner with organizations to extend your reach? Expand your client base by leveraging social media or referrals? Begin building systems to streamline operations as your business grows—whether that's automating invoicing, improving your workflow, or hiring support staff. Write down one strategy you can implement to grow your business.

The Shared Lesson: Embrace the Struggle

Tracy and Steve remind us that transformation is never easy. The leap from Educator to Entrepreneur—or any significant life change—is rarely smooth. There will be doubts, setbacks, and moments when the path forward feels impossibly hard.

But those struggles are where growth happens. Tracy's shaky first pitch taught her that confidence is built through action, not inaction. Steve's sleepless nights planning his first conference reminded him that perseverance is the bridge between vision and reality.

The journey may be difficult, but it's also deeply rewarding. It's about redefining what success looks like, stepping outside your comfort zone, and proving to yourself that you're capable of more than you ever imagined.

Remember: Struggle Means Growth

Struggle isn't a sign to stop; it's a sign you're growing. Just like Tracy, who transformed her shaky first pitch into a thriving coaching business, and Steve, who built an industry-changing conference model from the ground up, your challenges are the stepping stones to your transformation.

You already have what it takes to navigate this journey. The question is: Are you ready to take the next step? Whether you're just starting to dream or already building your legacy, the path forward is yours to shape.

Let's keep moving—one step, one goal, one mini-win, and one victory at a time.

Shared Lessons for All Professionals: Embracing the Struggle

The transition from a structured career to entrepreneurship or private practice is never without challenges. Coaches, therapists, and administrators all share common fears:

- "What if I fail?"
- "Will I attract enough clients?"
- "How do I manage the business side of things?"

These struggles are part of the process, and they're also opportunities for growth. Like Tracy's shaky first pitch and Steve's sleepless nights, your own moments of doubt will teach you resilience, adaptability, and perseverance.

Every step forward—no matter how small—is progress. By focusing on your strengths, leveraging your networks, and staying open to learning, you can transform your challenges into stepping stones toward success.

EXTENDED EDUCATOR

Expand Your Impact, Not Just Your Role

The edupreneurial mindset isn't just for classroom teachers—it's a strategy for anyone, in any role, ready to scale their impact.

- **Counselors:** You could design school-wide mental health programs, launch trauma-informed care workshops, or build community-based SEL resources.
- **Administrators:** Imagine taking your staff development approach and turning it into a statewide teacher recruitment and retention toolkit. That's what Pablo did. He shifted from running a school to supporting hundreds of leaders.
- **Coaches:** Create a youth sports app (it's easier and more cost-effective than you think), launch a training camp, or develop a "Coach-to-College" pipeline for underserved athletes.
- **SLPs/OTs/PTs:** Offer remote evaluations, build tools for educators to support diverse learners, or start a paid membership site for families navigating therapy.

You already have what it takes. The question isn't "can you?" It's "will you?"

Actionable Takeaways for Coaches, Therapists, and Administrators

1. Start Small and Build Trust:
   - Offer free or discounted trial sessions (coaches and therapists).
   - Start with small consulting projects or partnerships (administrators).
2. Leverage Tools and Resources:
   - Use software like TherapyNotes, SimplePractice, or scheduling platforms to simplify administrative tasks.
   - Invest in online courses or workshops to gain business skills tailored to your field.
3. Grow Your Network:
   - Connect with colleagues and attend industry events to generate referrals and build credibility.
   - Share your expertise through social media, blogs, or community events to establish authority in your niche.
4. Reframe Your Skills:
   - Focus on how your unique experiences—whether as a coach, therapist, or administrator—make you an asset in your new field.

Mini-Win:

Reflect on challenges you've overcome and the progress you've made. These wins are fuel for your next steps.

Reflection: Your Persona and Goals

Action Steps:

1. Identify Your Persona:
   Take a moment to reflect on which persona resonates with you the most right now: Educator, Embarker, or Entrepreneur. Understanding where you are will give you clarity about your next step.
2. Set One Goal:
   Write down one specific, actionable goal to help you move to the next persona.
   - Educator to Embarker: Research three industries where your skills might apply.
   - Embarker to Entrepreneur: Draft a simple business plan or test a side hustle idea.
   - Entrepreneur to Expansion: Identify one partnership opportunity or a way to scale your impact.

The journeys of Tracy and Steve remind us that stepping into uncharted territory takes courage, persistence, and a willingness to learn. Whether you're a coach, therapist, or administrator, you already have the tools to succeed—it's just a matter of taking the first step.

Let your passion guide you and remember that every struggle brings you closer to the transformation you're working toward. The best is yet to come.

Next Chapter, New Challenge: Learn, Lead, Leverage, Launch

In Chapter 5, we explored the three personas—Educator, Embarker, and Entrepreneur—and identified where you stand on your journey. But understanding your persona is only the beginning. Growth requires action, clarity, and strategy. Whether you're deeply rooted in the Educator role, exploring possibilities as an Embarker, or scaling your impact as an Entrepreneur, moving forward demands intention and courage.

This is where the **4-L Framework—Learn, Lead, Leverage, and Launch**—comes in.

CHAPTER 6: Navigating the Transition with the 4-L Framework – Learn, Lead, Leverage, Launch

Like scaffolding for a lesson plan, the 4-L Framework breaks your transformation into manageable phases, guiding you step by step toward success. Each phase builds upon the last, helping you align your skills, passions, and goals with the bold action required to navigate this transition.

Growth is rarely comfortable, but it is necessary. The familiar may feel safe, but it often limits your potential. As Charles Darwin said, **"It is not the strongest of the species that survives, nor the most intelligent, but the one most adaptable to change."** To evolve means to adapt, embrace discomfort, and move forward.

In this chapter, we'll not only break down the 4-L Framework but also revisit my journey and the stories of Tracy, Steve, and Charlotte to illustrate how these principles come to life in real-world transformations.

Learn: Acquiring Knowledge as the First Step to Commitment

Every journey begins with learning. This phase is about discovery—gathering information, building skills, and preparing for the road ahead.

For me, learning was the foundation of everything. Growing up in Little Havana during the crack epidemic of the 1990s, education became my escape route. My grandmother, a seamstress with a third-grade education, instilled in me a love of reading and a relentless drive to succeed. That love of learning led me to scholarships, college, and ultimately a doctorate in Educational Leadership.

But learning wasn't just about academics. When I left the structured world of education to pursue entrepreneurship, I realized that learning in this phase was different. It wasn't just about acquiring knowledge—it was about committing to a decision, burning the ships, and stepping fully into the unknown.

Tracy's story reflects this same phase. As a high school English teacher balancing financial pressures and caregiving for her mother, Tracy realized she needed to explore possibilities beyond the classroom. She attended webinars, joined writing workshops, and connected with others who had made similar transitions. Her curiosity and willingness to learn gave her the confidence to offer her first writing-coach session—a moment that marked the beginning of her transformation.

Lead: Stepping into Leadership with Total Commitment

Leadership begins with a decision to move forward. It's not just about guiding others; it's about leading yourself—trusting your instincts, embracing uncertainty, and stepping into uncharted territory.

When I transitioned from being a classroom educator to a sales executive with Holt, Rinehart, and Winston, I had to step into a new kind of leadership. I discovered how transferable my skills were—problem-solving, adaptability, and communication—but I also faced moments of doubt. Starting my tutoring company was another leap, one that required me to lead myself through fear and fully commit to my vision.

Steve Supe's journey exemplifies this phase. After decades as a superintendent and keynote speaker, Steve decided to challenge the traditional education conference model by creating a conference for educators, by educators. Leadership for Steve meant stepping away from the identity tied to his superintendent role and into the unknown. Despite his fears—Would people attend? Would vendors see the value?—he fully committed to his vision, embracing fear as fuel to drive him forward.

Ask Yourself:

- What fears are holding me back, and how can I reframe them as opportunities?
- What bold decision can I make today to lead myself toward my next goal?

Leverage: Maximizing What You've Built with No Escape Route

Leverage is where preparation meets action. It's about recognizing the value of your skills, experiences, and resources—and using them strategically to propel yourself forward.

When I built my tutoring company, I relied heavily on the leadership, organization, and empathy I had developed as an educator. Those same skills allowed me to scale the business to serve tens of thousands of students. Later, I applied those lessons to TeachTown, addressing a critical gap for children with autism. Each step of my journey built upon the last, proving that everything I had learned as a teacher was not just transferable—it was transformative.

Charlotte Charter's story echoes this principle. After years as a principal, Charlotte used her expertise in budgeting, staffing, and curriculum planning to launch her first charter school. She knew how to navigate the red tape of education systems, and she leveraged those skills to create a thriving learning environment. While securing funding and building trust within the community were challenges, Charlotte's ability to leverage her experience allowed her to overcome obstacles and grow her vision into a network of charter schools.

Leverage also requires a mindset shift. It's about recognizing that what you've built so far has immense value and trusting that you have what it takes to succeed.

Ask Yourself:

- What skills, experiences, or relationships can I leverage to move closer to my goal?
- How can I strategically apply these resources to gain momentum?

Launch: Embracing the Commitment and Moving into Uncharted Territory

The final phase of the 4-L Framework is Launch—the moment where preparation, leadership, and leverage converge. Launching is about action: fully committing to your vision, stepping into your new role, and scaling your impact.

For me, launching meant leaving behind the familiar safety of a secure job and taking the leap into entrepreneurship. The decision to build a tutoring company and later invest in TeachTown wasn't easy, but it was necessary. Each launch came with challenges, but the lessons learned at every step propelled me forward.

For **Tracy Tutor**, launching her writing-coach business was transformative. After months of preparing and building confidence, Tracy fully committed to her vision. She started small, working with just a handful of students, but her passion and expertise quickly became evident. As referrals rolled in, Tracy's business grew beyond what she had imagined. Today, she's earning twice her teaching salary, works fewer hours, and has the freedom to care for her mother while pursuing her own creative writing projects.

Launching isn't about having all the answers—it's about taking that first step.

Applying the Framework to Your Career Transition

Each quadrant of the 4-L Framework offers distinct opportunities for growth and transformation. **Learners** can prioritize building new skills through mentorships, training programs, or certifications that prepare them for the challenges ahead. **Leaders** have the chance to take bold, decisive steps—organizing teams, inspiring others, and establishing a clear vision for progress. **Leveragers** focus on maximizing existing resources—networks, expertise, and opportunities—to amplify their impact and scale their success. Finally, **Launchers** can channel their energy into executing visionary projects with confidence and purpose.

This framework goes beyond navigating career changes. It's about reshaping your narrative, embracing your potential, and stepping into your role as a transformative changemaker. By aligning the 4-L Framework with your unique persona and emotional readiness, you craft a personalized roadmap that leads to financial independence, personal growth, and professional fulfillment. It's not just about what you do—it's about who you become in the process.

Evolve or Die: The Urgency of Change

The 4-L Framework is a tool for evolution, but the choice to evolve begins with you. Holding on to familiar routines may feel comfortable, but in a world of constant change, stagnation is not an option. Change is inevitable; the real question is whether you'll adapt and thrive or be left behind.

Take **Pablo Principal**, for instance. A celebrated school principal deeply committed to his community, Pablo found himself teetering on the brink of burnout and financial instability. Despite his achievements and dedication, he faced a sobering truth: the system he had poured his heart and soul into wasn't providing enough for his family's future or his personal well-being.

Pablo's evolution wasn't easy, but it was essential. He acknowledged his worth, took decisive steps to redefine his career, and transitioned into a leadership consulting role that not only honored his expertise but also offered financial security and personal fulfillment. Leveraging his years of experience managing school systems and mentoring teachers, Pablo built a consultancy focused on leadership development for school administrators. Today, he's thriving, impacting school districts across the country and creating a legacy he once only dreamed of.

Pablo's journey, like so many others, highlights an important truth: growth demands courage and action. The decision to evolve is deeply personal, but it's also profoundly empowering. The 4-L Framework can guide your path, offering tools and strategies for transformation, but the first step—choosing to embrace change and step into the future—is yours alone.

A Story of Evolution: Pablo Principal and the 4-L Framework

Pablo Principal was the embodiment of dedication and purpose. As a principal, he poured his heart into his school and community, becoming a beacon of leadership and inspiration. His staff

admired his vision, his students thrived under his care, and parents trusted him to care for their children and guide the school toward excellence. Yet beneath the awards and accolades was a man grappling with a painful truth: He was burnt-out and financially insecure.

Pablo carried the weight of the "3 Ps"—Poor, Pissed-Off, and Proud.

- Poor because his role, despite its prestige, could not provide the financial stability his family desperately needed after his spouse lost her job.
- Pissed-Off at a system that demanded so much yet gave so little in return, leaving him overworked, undervalued, and unable to secure a future for his family.
- Proud of the work he had done, the lives he had impacted, and the change he had fostered in his school and community.

Despite his achievements, Pablo faced a sobering reality - with his spouse out of work and foreclosure looming, he was forced to confront the limitations of his current role. A celebrated principal—the cornerstone of his community—was now fighting to keep his family afloat.

Faced with a choice—continue to endure or find the courage to evolve—Pablo's journey through the 4-L Framework began.

Learn: Building the Foundation

Pablo's first step was to Learn. He knew that staying in his current role, no matter how fulfilling it had once been, would not solve his financial problems or reignite the passion he had lost. He began researching opportunities outside the traditional school system, focusing on areas where his skills could make the greatest impact.

Drawing on his experience as a teacher and administrator, Pablo realized his expertise working with English Language Learners

(ELL) compliance was an untapped asset. His superb track record of ensuring Limited English Proficiency (LEP) Plans were not only met but exceeded had earned him a reputation for excellence. He identified a growing need in the charter school market for leaders who understood both the complexities of compliance and the importance of serving English Language Learners.

Through workshops, mentorships, and market research, Pablo began to see how his skills could translate into a broader role. Learning wasn't just about gaining knowledge—it was about realizing his value and recognizing the opportunities available to him.

Lead: Taking Bold Action

Pablo's opportunity to lead himself into a new chapter came when a national charter school organization reached out with an offer. They were expanding rapidly and needed someone to oversee ELL compliance across their growing network of schools. It was a daunting role, with responsibility for thousands of students and teachers. The organization needed a leader with both a deep understanding of compliance and the vision to scale their operations effectively.

At first, Pablo hesitated. Could he leave behind his school community, the teachers he had mentored, and the students he had watched grow? Could he navigate the complexities of a national organization and the demands of a role so far outside his comfort zone?

These doubts were compounded by the biggest challenge of his career: negotiating a compensation package that reflected his worth. As a career educator, he had never been in a position to advocate for his own salary. But Pablo knew this was his moment to lead—not just for his career but for his family's future.

He meticulously prepared for the negotiation, outlining his achievements, the programs he had implemented, and the measurable impact he had made. When the time came, he confidently presented his case. His boldness paid off: the organization offered him a salary and benefits package that far exceeded his expectations. For the first time, Pablo felt valued not just as an educator but as a leader.

Leverage: Maximizing His Strengths

Stepping into his new role as a leader in the charter school organization, Pablo immediately faced challenges. Scaling ELL programs across a national network required navigating complex legal frameworks, training staff in compliance, and building systems to ensure consistent quality.

Pablo leaned into the strengths he had honed as a principal. His ability to inspire trust, foster collaboration, and execute a vision became invaluable. He introduced innovative training programs for teachers, streamlined compliance processes, and created systems to monitor and support LEP Plan implementation across hundreds of schools.

Pablo also leveraged his reputation as a results-driven leader. By highlighting his successes and building relationships with stakeholders, he gained the trust of his team and the broader organization. He worked closely with teachers, administrators, and families to ensure that the needs of ELL students were not just met but prioritized.

His efforts led to measurable improvements in compliance rates, student outcomes, and teacher satisfaction. Pablo's leadership proved that a commitment to equity and excellence could drive success on a national scale.

Launch: Thriving and Redefining Success

Within a few years, Pablo had launched into a position of extraordinary influence. He was overseeing not just ELL but the academic performance of hundreds of thousands of students nationwide. His leadership transformed the organization, setting new standards for compliance, innovation, and student achievement.

Today, Pablo's work impacts students and teachers across the country, particularly those in ELL classrooms, and is a leading voice for the transformative power of parental choice and charter schools. Under his leadership, the organization has become a model for how charter schools can effectively serve diverse learners. Beyond professional success, Pablo has secured financial stability for his family, allowing him to focus on what matters most: building a legacy of impact and equity in education.

A Testament to Courage and Self-Worth

Pablo Principal's story illustrates the transformative power of the 4-L Framework. His journey began with **Learning**—gaining the knowledge and self-awareness to see new possibilities. It progressed to **Leading**—taking bold action to advocate for his worth and embrace change. He then **Leveraged** his strengths to excel in his new role, and finally, he **Launched** into a future filled with impact, purpose, and fulfillment.

Pablo's courage serves as a powerful reminder to us all. When we align our actions with our true worth and embrace the 4-L Framework, we unlock opportunities to thrive in ways we never imagined. His story proves that evolution isn't just possible—it's necessary. All it takes is the courage to begin.

EXTENDED EDUCATOR

Four Ls, One Leap

Let's break it down—*Learn, Lead, Leverage, Launch* isn't just for teachers pivoting to business, it's a roadmap for any of us who've outgrown our lane.

You've already done *Learn*. You've got the degrees, the certifications, the hours of PD that would impress any board.

You've done *Lead*, even if you don't wear the title. Every time you coach a kid through a tough season or guide a family through an emotional breakthrough—that's leadership.

So now? It's time to *Leverage*. Take what you've built and ask: how can I scale this? Package it? Price it?

And then, *Launch*. Not with perfection, but with intention.

You don't need to overhaul your life overnight. You just need to move one "L" forward at a time. The only thing missing is action.

Mini-Win:

Identify one area where adaptability is crucial for your growth. Write down one step you'll take this week to develop that skill or mindset.

Action Steps:

The 4-L Framework is a guide to transformation, but its power lies in your willingness to act. Take these steps one at a time, adapting them to your unique journey. With each action, you'll move closer to your goals and unlock your full potential. Start today—the future you envision begins with the courage to take the first step.

The 4-L Framework and Action Steps

Step	Action Example
Learn	Identify gaps in your knowledge and seek new skills.
Lead	Apply what you've learned to forge your path.
Leverage	Maximize your strengths to create new opportunities.
Launch	Take bold, decisive action to bring your vision to life.

Identify an Area for Growth:

Write down one key area where you need to adapt or improve to thrive in your transition. Be honest with yourself about what's holding you back or where you could use support.

Examples:

- Time Management: Balancing priorities during a demanding transition.
- Financial Planning: Gaining clarity on your financial goals and resources.
- Networking: Expanding your professional connections to create new opportunities.
- Skill Development: Learning a new tool or refining your expertise for a new role.

Research a Resource:

Once you've identified an area for growth, look for resources that can help you take the next step. This could be a course, book, podcast, workshop, or mentorship opportunity.

Examples:

- For time management: Explore productivity tools like Getting Things Done by David Allen[2] or a time-blocking course.
- For financial planning: Consider a session with a financial coach or read *The Total Money Makeover* by Dave Ramsey[3].
- For networking: Join a professional organization or attend a virtual industry meetup.
- For skill development: Enroll in a certification course or watch tutorials on platforms like Coursera, Udemy, or LinkedIn Learning.

Commit to One Action This Week:

Set a small, actionable goal to move closer to your larger objective. Choose something specific and achievable that aligns with your current stage in the 4-L Framework.

Examples:

- If you're in the Learn stage: Schedule 30 minutes daily to read or complete an online module.
- If you're in the Lead stage: Write a script to advocate for yourself in a salary negotiation or career conversation.
- If you're in the Leverage stage: Reach out to a mentor or colleague to discuss how you can maximize your current resources.
- If you're in the Launch stage: Begin executing one aspect of your vision, whether it's drafting a proposal or implementing a new strategy.

Next Chapter, New Challenge: Seize the Moment

Chapter 6 took us through the transformative journey of the 4-L Framework—Learning, Leading, Leveraging, and Launching. It's a process that allowed individuals like Pablo Principal, Tracy

Tutor, Steve Supe, and Charlotte Charter to break free from limitations, embrace growth, and step into their next chapters with purpose and clarity.

For Pablo, leveraging his deep understanding of ELL compliance elevated him from a school building to the national stage, where he now oversees a charter network serving hundreds of thousands of students. Tracy reimagined her classroom expertise to build a thriving business that provides her with flexibility and fulfillment. Steve challenged the status quo of education conferences, turning an outdated model into a platform that empowers leaders. And Charlotte took her experience as a school principal and scaled it into a nationwide network of successful charter schools.

What ties these stories together isn't just the steps they took—it's the mindset they adopted along the way. Growth begins with action, but it's sustained by how you think and how you approach the inevitable challenges that come with reinvention. They didn't let fear or uncertainty stop them. Instead, they reframed challenges as opportunities, embraced creativity, and made bold, strategic choices that aligned with their visions for the future.

Now, it's your turn to make that shift. Chapter 7 is about embracing the **entrepreneurial mindset**—the key to seizing opportunity, unlocking potential, and thriving in the face of uncertainty.

PART 3:

Breaking the Bell: Your Next Chapter in Business and Beyond

CHAPTER 7:

Seize the Moment- Adopting the Entrepreneur Mindset for Success

The entrepreneurial mindset isn't reserved for CEOs or startup founders. It's a way of thinking that allows you to approach challenges creatively, think strategically, and make deliberate decisions that move you closer to your vision. It's about recognizing that obstacles are opportunities in disguise and that resilience is built through action.

For **Pablo Principal**, adopting this mindset meant stepping away from the security of his school community and into a corporate leadership role with a national charter school organization. Pablo didn't know what awaited him, but he recognized an opportunity to serve students on a broader scale, particularly those learning English. His success didn't come from knowing everything upfront—it came from a commitment to learning, leading, and pushing forward, even when the path was unclear.

Similarly, **Tracy Tutor's** journey as a writing coach began with uncertainty. She didn't know if her skills would translate into a viable business, but she embraced the entrepreneurial mindset, taking action even when it felt imperfect. That willingness to act gave her clarity, confidence, and the momentum to grow her business into a fulfilling career that supported her family.

The entrepreneurial mindset is rooted in a simple but powerful truth: **you don't have to have all the answers to take the first step.** Action creates clarity. You learn, adapt, and grow by doing. This mindset is about embracing that process—reframing fear, thinking creatively, and pushing forward with purpose.

Cultivating the Entrepreneurial Mindset

Adopting this mindset starts with a decision: to step outside your comfort zone and see every challenge as an opportunity to innovate. It's not about being fearless—it's about acting in spite of fear. For **Steve Supe**, it was deciding that the outdated education conference model didn't have to define the future. For **Charlotte Charter**, it was taking the leap to scale one school into a network that served thousands. Both understood that uncertainty wasn't the enemy–stagnation was.

This mindset allows you to reframe obstacles as stepping stones and to see opportunities that others overlook. It sharpens your ability to problem-solve, adapt, and move forward no matter what lies ahead.

Your Moment Is Now

This is the moment to embrace that shift—to stop waiting for the perfect conditions and start creating them. The entrepreneurial mindset will help you move through uncertainty with confidence and purpose. It will give you the tools to think strategically, act boldly, and bounce back stronger when you encounter setbacks.

In this chapter, we'll explore how to make this mindset part of your daily approach. Together, we'll unpack the strategies that will help you cultivate creativity, build resilience, and make deliberate choices that align with your goals. The individuals we've met—Pablo, Tracy, Steve, and Charlotte—are living proof of what's possible when you think boldly and act with intention.

The path ahead is filled with opportunities waiting to be seized. The only question is: will you take the first step? Let's move forward together and embrace the mindset that will empower you to create the future you deserve.

My Bold Leap: From The Education Doctor to TeachTown

The entrepreneurial mindset isn't just about thinking differently—it's about acting decisively, committing fully, and embracing the risks and rewards of innovation. For me, this mindset became my compass as I transitioned from running The Education Doctor to investing and joining TeachTown, a move that redefined my career and solidified my identity as an edupreneur.

The shift from building a successful tutoring company to becoming part of a mission-driven organization like TeachTown wasn't just a career pivot—it was a leap of faith into uncharted territory. Having scaled The Education Doctor to serve tens of thousands of students, I believed I had found my purpose: providing equitable educational opportunities for underserved students.

But as I took a deeper look into the educational landscape, a glaring need became impossible to ignore. Students with autism spectrum disorders (ASD) were being underserved—both in classrooms and at home. Despite their potential, these students lacked the tools, resources, and support systems they needed to thrive. This realization was my call to action—one that pushed me to think beyond tutoring and into creating innovative solutions for a population that had been overlooked.

The Leap into TeachTown

TeachTown presented the opportunity to answer that call. Its mission of designing tools for teachers, therapists, and parents to better support students with ASD aligned perfectly with my drive to make a lasting impact. But this leap wasn't just about joining a company with a compelling mission—it was about truly owning it.

Like Steve Supe, who invested his time and vision into reinventing education conferences, I knew that belief alone wasn't enough. I didn't just take a seat at the table; I took real, personal stakes in its success. My belief in its mission was so strong that I made a significant financial investment to become part of the company. This wasn't just about faith—it was about accountability. By tying my own resources directly to TeachTown's outcomes, I wasn't simply investing in a company; I was committing to its success on the deepest level. Failure wasn't an option—I was, once again, burning the ships and eliminating any path of retreat.

I had to give everything I had to ensure its growth, knowing the stakes extended far beyond the students we aimed to serve. This decision was about my family, my future, and my unwavering belief in the transformative power of education.

The leap from The Education Doctor to TeachTown wasn't just a professional move; it was a defining moment in my life. It required courage, clarity, and a willingness to bet on myself and my vision for what education could become. It also forced me to confront fear head-on. What if this didn't work? What if I lost everything? These questions were constant companions, but so was the answer: I had built a foundation strong enough to weather any challenge.

The skills I had honed over the years—scaling a business, building relationships, and leading with empathy—became my anchors. My experience as an educator helped me understand the needs of students with autism, while my entrepreneurial journey gave me the confidence to navigate the complexities of growing a business. Despite my preparation, the fear of failure was real. But retreat wasn't an option. I was all in, and the only path was forward.

Charlotte Charter taught us the power of scaling a vision. She took a single school and grew it into a network, leveraging her expertise in curriculum design and leadership. Similarly, I leaned on my experience in scaling The Education Doctor to understand how to grow a business while maintaining its mission.

At TeachTown, I poured everything I had into the mission. The hours were long, the work demanding, and the challenges often overwhelming. But every late night, every brainstorming session, and every collaboration with educators reminded me why I had taken this leap. This wasn't just about creating tools; it was about solving a deeply personal and societal issue. Every skill I had cultivated, every connection I had nurtured, and every lesson I had learned came into play.

The fear of failure was ever present. What if I couldn't grow TeachTown? What if I let down the students and educators who depended on us? What if I lost everything? These questions loomed large, but I wasn't alone in this struggle.

Pablo overcame his doubts by trusting in his ability to adapt and learn. Tracy embraced the discomfort of her first pitch, knowing that forward motion—no matter how small—was progress. And like Frida Finance, who transitioned into a role supporting education ventures, I reminded myself that fear wasn't a signal to stop; it was a sign that I was stepping into something meaningful.

I knew the stakes were high—not just for TeachTown, but for the students, families, and educators who depended on us. This leap was more than a career move; it was a commitment to redefining what's possible in education. And just like every bold leap, it demanded unwavering focus, relentless determination, and the belief that forward momentum, no matter how small, would lead to meaningful change.

This chapter in my journey taught me that embracing the entrepreneurial mindset isn't just about starting something new—it's about stepping fully into the unknown with the confidence that your purpose, preparation, and passion will guide you through.

A Critical Mindset Shift

This leap wasn't just about financial or professional risk; it required a fundamental shift in how I saw myself and my work. It wasn't enough to embrace the entrepreneurial mindset—I had to redefine my identity within it. I had to stop seeing this move as a departure from education and start recognizing it as an expansion of my impact.

The skills I had cultivated over years as a teacher and leader—empathy, communication, adaptability, and problem-solving—weren't just relevant in the entrepreneurial space; they were essential. These were the same skills that allowed me to connect with students, inspire colleagues, and solve real-world challenges in the classroom. Now, they were helping me design innovative tools, foster meaningful relationships, and navigate the complexities of scaling a mission-driven company.

This realization redefined what it meant to me to be an **edupreneur**—*an innovator who bridges the worlds of education and entrepreneurship to create meaningful, scalable solutions that address pressing educational challenges.*

Being an edupreneur isn't about leaving one world behind; it's about building a bridge between what you know and what's possible. It's about stepping into the discomfort of growth, leaning into uncertainty, and trusting that your past experiences have equipped you to tackle the unknown. It's about realizing that everything you've done up until now has prepared you for this moment—and that the impact you can make is only limited by the boundaries you're willing to break.

This shift wasn't easy. It required me to challenge the stories I had told myself about what success looked like and to embrace the idea that I could define it on my own terms. But once I did, everything changed. I stopped seeing myself as "just" a teacher or a leader and started seeing myself as a creator, an innovator, and an agent of change.

And that's the mindset shift I hope to inspire in you. The leap isn't about leaving behind your purpose; it's about discovering how far it can reach when you trust yourself enough to take it.

From Risk to Reward

Eventually, the hard work paid off. TeachTown grew into a company that fundamentally changed how students with autism were supported, both in schools and at home. Our tools became invaluable resources, helping to create inclusive environments where these students could thrive.

When TeachTown was acquired by Bain Capital, it was more than a professional milestone—it was a deeply personal validation of the years of resilience, dedication, and belief in a mission that mattered.

But the true reward wasn't financial. It wasn't even professional. It was knowing that our work was making a difference—seeing students progress, hearing parents' gratitude, and empowering educators to better serve their students. That's what made the risks worth it.

Lessons for the Leap Ahead

This journey taught me that success requires full commitment—not halfway, not "if it works out." The moment I invested in TeachTown, financially and emotionally, there was no going back.

That commitment made all the difference.

Like Charlotte scaling her schools or Pablo redefining his role in education leadership, I learned that resilience is built in the moments when everything feels like it's falling apart. The struggle isn't a detour—it's the forge that shapes your skills and sharpens your resolve.

And just like Tracy, who found fulfillment through imperfect action, I realized that forward momentum doesn't require certainty—it requires courage.

Resilience is built in the moments when everything feels like it's falling apart. The struggle isn't a roadblock; it's the forge that sharpens your skills and strengthens your resolve. And the true measure of success isn't in titles or paychecks; it's in the lives you impact and the change you create.

I learned that embracing the entrepreneurial mindset is about trusting yourself enough to take the leap and betting on your ability to make a difference. If you're standing on the edge of your own leap, know this: you're ready. The path ahead will challenge you, but it will also shape you into more than you ever imagined.

The leap isn't about leaving your purpose behind; it's about discovering just how far it can take you.

What it Means to Take a Leap in Edupreneurship

Edupreneurship is about more than just creating something new—it's about transforming what's possible, even in the face of systemic challenges. It's about seeing where others see limits, using your skills and experiences as building blocks, and trusting yourself to take risks despite uncertainty.

For Pablo Principal, his venture into edupreneurship wasn't about leaving behind his role as a school administrator—it was about expanding his impact. By stepping into the leadership of a national charter network, he amplified his expertise in ELL, reaching hundreds of thousands of students and teachers. Pablo's leap taught him that edupreneurship is about scaling what you already do well to serve on a broader stage, even when fear whispers that you're stepping into the unknown.

The Weight of the Unknown

That doesn't mean the path is easy—it's not. There were moments when the challenges felt overwhelming. I questioned my decisions, wrestled with self-doubt, and wondered if I had made the right move. These weren't fleeting thoughts; they were constant companions during late nights and uphill battles. But those moments were also the most defining. They pushed me to lean into discomfort, to problem-solve in new ways, and to remind myself of the "why" behind my leap.

When I think of Tracy Tutor, I remember how she began her writing-coach journey with just one nervous pitch to a parent. Tracy didn't have a polished business plan or a perfect strategy—she had a willingness to try and the resilience to learn. That same resilience became her anchor as she grew her business into something fulfilling and impactful.

The challenges I faced with TeachTown were different but no less demanding. Like Tracy, I had to build something from the ground up. I poured everything I had into promoting and selling tools that would make life better for students with autism, their families, and their educators. And when the obstacles felt impossible to overcome, I reminded myself that this was bigger than me.

The True Rewards of Edupreneurship

Edupreneurship isn't about chasing financial success, though financial stability is often part of the reward. The deeper rewards are the ones that remind you why you took the leap in the first place. It's hearing a parent say, "This program changed everything for my child." It's watching a teacher use your solution to connect with a student who had been unreachable. It's knowing that you provided something that didn't exist before—something that solves a problem, meets a need, or makes someone's life better.

Steve Supe experienced this firsthand when he reinvented the education conference model. By creating a conference for educators, by educators, he didn't just fill a gap—he created a thriving platform that gave leaders across the country tools and inspiration to bring back to their districts. Steve's leap into edupreneurship wasn't just about conferences—it was about creating a system that empowered educators to lead change.

The rewards, like Steve's and mine, go far beyond professional achievements. They're about impact. They're about creating something lasting and meaningful that solves real problems.

Edupreneurship as a Catalyst for Change

Edupreneurship is about taking everything you know—your skills, your experiences, your passions—and using them to create something transformative. It's about pushing boundaries, meeting needs, and opening doors where there were none before.

Take Charlotte Charter, for example. Charlotte didn't stop at creating one excellent school. She scaled her expertise, growing a network of schools that now serve thousands of students. Like Charlotte, when you leap into edupreneurship, you're not just solving problems on a small scale—you're building something that can ripple out, impacting communities far beyond your immediate reach.

The Path Forward

If you're considering your own leap into edupreneurship, know this: it will challenge you in ways you can't yet imagine. It will test your resilience, demand your focus, and force you to step outside of your comfort zone. But it will also grow you, shape you, and show you what you're capable of when you lean into your vision with courage and commitment.

The path isn't always clear, but clarity often comes from taking the first step. Like Frida, who leveraged her financial expertise to support educational initiatives, or Tracy, who redefined her classroom skills into a thriving business, you'll find that action creates momentum.

The leap into edupreneurship isn't just about creating something for yourself—it's about creating something that can change lives. It's about betting on yourself, your vision, and your ability to make an impact. It's about trusting that the challenges you've faced up to this point have prepared you for the ones ahead.

The world of education, with all its complexities and challenges, needs more people willing to take that leap. Because when you do, you're not just stepping into your next chapter—you're shaping the future for students, teachers, and communities who need innovative solutions and bold leadership.

You're ready for the leap. And the rewards—both seen and unseen—will be worth every step.

Lessons from Risk-Taking

Edupreneurship isn't about perfection—it's about persistence, adaptability, and staying purpose- driven. It's about approaching each step as an opportunity to learn and grow, even when the path feels uncertain. Tools like the entrepreneurial mindset checklist can serve as a guide, but ultimately, your journey will be uniquely yours, shaped by your goals, your challenges, and your willingness to embrace risk.

For me, the leap from The Education Doctor to TeachTown wasn't just about creating a new career path—it was about aligning my work with my mission to transform education for underserved students. It wasn't only about financial rewards, though they were part of the outcome; it was about achieving a deeper kind of freedom—the freedom to create something meaningful that could have a lasting impact.

Like Pablo Principal, who left the security of his school to lead a charter network, my leap was rooted in a purpose larger than myself. And like Tracy Tutor, who faced her fears to grow a business from a single client, I learned that growth comes from taking deliberate, purposeful action—even when the outcome is uncertain.

Cultivating the Entrepreneurial Mindset

The entrepreneurial mindset isn't a fixed trait; it's a skillset you develop through practice, persistence, and a commitment to action. It's about trusting in your ability to navigate the unknown, embracing the lessons that come with risk, and staying focused on the purpose driving your decisions.

Your leap begins with the steps you take today. Each small action builds momentum, bringing you closer to your goals and helping you create something bigger than yourself—something that can change lives.

A Transformative Mindset

The entrepreneurial mindset empowers you to look beyond your current role and see the possibilities for innovation, growth, and impact. It's not about leaving education behind—it's about taking what you know and using it to create something bigger, something that truly transforms lives.

Whether you're a counselor, an administrator, a coach, or a therapist, your skills are already valuable. The challenge is reimagining how they can be applied to serve more people, solve bigger problems, and create lasting change.

The path isn't easy, but it's worth it. Just as Frida Finance found her purpose supporting education ventures, you, too, can use your expertise to redefine what's possible. The world of education is waiting for bold thinkers, innovative leaders, and passionate problem-solvers ready to take the leap.

Your journey begins today—with one bold risk, one meaningful step, and one unwavering belief in your ability to create something extraordinary. What will your next step be?

EXTENDED EDUCATOR

You Don't Need More Time—You Need More Truth

Let me guess. You've told yourself you'll make the leap when things "settle down."

But let me ask you something real: **When has your job ever settled down?**

If you're a principal, a mental health professional, or an SLP juggling three schools, the chaos isn't a season—it's the system. So stop waiting for the perfect moment, because, spoiler alert, that moment doesn't exist. What does exist is *right now.*

One idea you've had on the backburner. One Saturday you block off for strategy instead of spreadsheets. One DM you send to a potential collaborator instead of scrolling LinkedIn in silence.

Momentum doesn't come from motivation—it comes from movement.

And your moment? It isn't ahead of you. It's already here.

Mini-Win: Ignite Your Progress

Your entrepreneurial journey begins with the risks you're willing to take. What will your bold move be this month? Write it down, share it, and take one step to bring it to life. Let that action be the spark that ignites your progress.

Action Steps:

Bold risks don't happen overnight—they're the result of small, intentional steps that build confidence, momentum, and clarity. Here's how you can start putting the entrepreneurial mindset into motion:

1. **Write Down One Bold Risk:** Identify one bold risk you're willing to take this month to move closer to your goals. Maybe it's pitching an idea to your school district, launching a new side hustle, applying for a leadership role, or investing in a professional development course. Writing it down makes it tangible and gives you a clear target to aim for.
2. **Share Your Idea with Someone You Trust:** Share your plan with a mentor, colleague, or friend. Steve Supe leaned heavily on his network to refine his vision for education conferences, and their feedback helped him create something revolutionary. Similarly, sharing your idea can provide accountability, open the door to fresh perspectives, and remind you that you're not alone.
3. **Take One Action:** Take a concrete step, no matter how small. It could be sending an email, drafting an outline, or signing up for that course you've been considering. As Charlotte Charter showed us when she scaled her first school into a network, momentum builds through consistent action, turning small steps into transformational progress.

The Power of Small Steps

These small actions might not feel like much in the moment, but they lay the foundation for big changes. Writing down your risk clarifies your focus, sharing your idea builds support, and taking action turns your vision into reality.

Remember, every bold leap starts with a single step. What risk will you take today to move closer to the life and impact you've been dreaming of?

The Entrepreneurial Mindset Checklist

Step	Action Example	Example
Commit to Growth	Be willing to learn new skills and adapt.	Enroll in a course on business strategy or attend a workshop on innovation.
Embrace Risk	Accept that uncertainty is part of progress.	Pitch your idea to a new audience, even if you're unsure of the outcome.
Leverage Your Strengths	Identify how your current skills translate to new opportunities.	Use your teaching experience to create an online training program.
Take Bold Action	Start before you feel ready.	Launch your pilot program or product and refine it as you go.

Next Chapter, New Challenge: F.R.E.E.D.O.M. Formula

Chapter 7 challenged you to adopt the entrepreneurial mindset—a way of thinking that transforms challenges into opportunities and turns uncertainty into growth. We explored how individuals like Pablo Principal, Tracy Tutor, and Steve Supe leaned into this mindset to overcome doubt, reimagine their potential, and create impact far beyond their initial roles. But adopting the mindset is just the beginning.

Having the vision to take bold risks is essential, but the next step is turning that vision into a systematic plan—one that aligns your goals with actionable strategies. This is where the **F.R.E.E.D.O.M. Formula comes into play.**

CHAPTER 8:

F.R.E.E.D.O.M. Formula – Unlocking Your Path to Financial Independence

The word *freedom* carries a powerful weight, and its meaning is deeply personal. For some, freedom is about escaping financial strain, paying off debt, or creating a secure future for their family. For others, it's about reclaiming their time, energy, and ability to pursue passions, spend more time with loved ones, or leave a lasting legacy.

Regardless of how you define it, freedom boils down to one essential idea: **the ability to design a life aligned with your values and goals.**

When I transitioned from The Education Doctor to TeachTown, my own definition of freedom evolved. At first, it was about financial independence, but as the journey unfolded, I realized it was also about creating impact—building something that solved real problems and made life better for others. Whether it's the freedom to create, innovate, or lead, what we're ultimately seeking is a life that aligns with our deepest values.

That's where the **F.R.E.E.D.O.M. Formula comes** in. This blueprint—**Focus, Reflect, Evaluate, Engage, Develop, Organize, Motivate**—isn't just a collection of ideas. It's a practical, actionable system designed to help you take control of your finances, career, and future.

In this chapter, we'll break down each component of the F.R.E.E.D.O.M. Formula with real stories, actionable steps, and tools you can use to implement these principles in your own journey. You'll learn how to focus on what matters most, reflect on where you are and where you want to go, and evaluate opportunities with clarity and confidence. You'll engage with the people and resources that can propel you forward, develop the skills you need to succeed, organize your actions into a clear plan, and stay motivated through every step of the process.

By the end of this chapter, you'll have a clear understanding of how to apply the F.R.E.E.D.O.M. Formula **to** your own journey. Whether you're looking to break free from financial stress, pivot to a new career, or scale your impact, this formula will guide you every step of the way.

The freedom you're seeking isn't some far-off dream—it's a goal that begins with the actions you take today. Let's break it down, step by step, and unlock the life you've been working toward. Because your freedom isn't just possible—it's within reach. Let's get started.

Focus: Clarity is Power

For Pablo Principal, a celebrated school leader grappling with financial instability, clarity became his guiding force. Like many education administrators, Pablo had poured his heart into his school and community, leading with dedication and purpose. But when his spouse lost her job, and the threat of foreclosure loomed, he found himself questioning everything. The pressures of his professional and personal life collided, leaving him feeling stuck, and overwhelmed by uncertainty.

Pablo's turning point came late one evening after a particularly challenging day. Desperate for direction, he grabbed a notebook and began writing. At first, his thoughts were scattered, but as he continued, one question emerged: **What do I really want?** The answer wasn't immediate, but as he reflected, he realized his passion wasn't tied solely to his current role—it was in empowering schools and educators on a larger scale.

This clarity became Pablo's compass. He outlined a plan to transition from his current position to a leadership role that allowed him to impact education systems nationwide while providing financial security for his family. Each step, though small, moved him closer to his goal.

Pablo's journey shows us that clarity isn't just a mindset—it's a tool. It simplifies complexity, quiets self-doubt, and turns overwhelming challenges into purposeful actions. By focusing on what truly matters, you can break free from uncertainty and take meaningful steps toward a future aligned with your vision.

Clarity transformed Pablo's uncertainty into determination. The result? A leadership role that not only aligned with his passion but also provided financial security and flexibility for his family. His journey illustrates a vital truth: **clarity isn't just a mindset—it's a tool.** It simplifies complexity, quiets self-doubt, and turns overwhelming challenges into purposeful actions.

Actionable Tip: Write down one financial or career goal for this year. Break it into quarterly milestones. For example:

- Quarter 1: Draft a business plan or resume tailored to your goals.

- Quarter 2: Build three meaningful connections in your target industry.
- Quarter 3: Test a new opportunity, like a side hustle or freelance project.
- Quarter 4: Expand on your progress by scaling or adding new services.

Reflect: Progress Requires Perspective

For Stephanie Sped, a special education teacher turned school founder, reflection wasn't just a strategy—it became her lifeline during the chaotic early days of building her school. Like many new edupreneurs, Stephanie found herself overwhelmed by the sheer volume of challenges.

Fundraising efforts were coming up short, parents voiced skepticism about her vision, and the constant turnover of staff made building a cohesive team feel nearly impossible.

Amid the chaos, Stephanie developed a habit that transformed her approach. Every Friday evening, after the school had emptied and the noise of the week had quieted, she sat alone with a notebook and reflected. She would jot down the week's successes and struggles, asking herself key questions:

- What went well?
- What didn't?
- What needs attention next week?

At first, the practice served as an outlet for her frustrations, but over time, it became something far more powerful: a roadmap for growth. Reflection helped Stephanie uncover insights she wouldn't have noticed otherwise. She identified which fundraising strategies were worth doubling down on and which weren't. Parent concerns became opportunities for better communication and community engagement. Patterns in staff feedback allowed her to develop strategies for improving retention and morale.

What started as a coping mechanism grew into a systematic tool for progress. Week by week, Stephanie's reflections revealed her next steps, keeping her grounded and focused on her ultimate mission. These small, consistent adjustments had a profound impact. Within a few years, Stephanie's school became a beacon of success, known for its innovative approach to serving students with unique needs.

Stephanie's journey demonstrates that **progress doesn't come from doing more—it comes from doing better.** Reflection is the tool that turns challenges into opportunities and chaos into clarity. It's not just about identifying what went wrong—it's about recognizing what's working, learning from the experience, and using those insights to make purposeful decisions.

Whether it's a weekly reflection like Stephanie's or a brief pause at the end of each day, taking time to reflect gives you the perspective to see progress, even in incremental steps. It helps you stay connected to your purpose and adjust your actions to achieve long-term success.

Actionable Tip: Create a weekly journaling habit to guide your reflection. Use these prompts to get started:

- What went well this week?
- What challenges did I face?
- What can I improve next week?

Reflection is more than a look back—it's a way forward. Like Stephanie, it can become the cornerstone of your growth and success.

Evaluate: Stop Being Busy; Start Being Effective

For Cathy Counselor, transitioning from high school counseling to private coaching was fueled by passion—but passion alone wasn't enough to sustain her. Cathy believed sheer effort would drive her success, so she tackled every task head-on. But instead of progress, she found herself exhausted and overwhelmed by busywork.

Her breakthrough came when she conducted a **time audit,** tracking how she spent every hour of her workday for two weeks. The results were shocking: nearly 60% of her time was spent on tasks like emails and administrative work—tasks that, while necessary, weren't moving her business forward.

With this realization, Cathy reevaluated her approach. She hired a virtual assistant to handle scheduling and administrative tasks, freeing her to focus on high-impact activities like building client relationships, creating coaching programs, and marketing her services. This shift not only reignited her passion but also led to significant growth in her practice.

Cathy's story is a powerful reminder: **being busy isn't the same as being effective.** Evaluating how you spend your time—and making deliberate changes—allows you to shift from reactive busyness to purposeful action.

Actionable Tip: Review last week's calendar. Highlight tasks that advanced your goals and identify low-value tasks to delegate or automate. Ask yourself:

- What deserves my full attention?
- What can I delegate or eliminate?

Engage: Relationships Are Everything

For Stephanie Sped, networking didn't come naturally. As a special education teacher turned school founder, she initially felt isolated in her new role. She quickly realized that she couldn't build her vision alone—she needed mentors, collaborators, and advocates to help her navigate the complexities of leadership and growth.

Her first industry conference felt daunting. Stephanie was surrounded by seasoned professionals, and self-doubt crept in. But instead of retreating, she decided to engage. She approached a speaker whose insights about innovative school leadership resonated with her. That one conversation led to a mentorship that would shape her journey. Through this mentor, Stephanie gained invaluable advice, was introduced to key stakeholders, and built partnerships that propelled her school's success.

Engagement isn't just about collecting business cards or adding connections on LinkedIn—it's about building authentic, meaningful relationships. In my own journey, I've seen the transformative power of relationships. When I transitioned from The Education Doctor to TeachTown, I leaned heavily on my network of educators, parents, and industry experts to better understand the unique needs of students with autism. These connections not only shaped the tools we developed but also opened doors to partnerships and opportunities that accelerated our mission.

Success in edupreneurship isn't just about what you know—it's about **who you know** and how you collaborate to create meaningful impact. Engaging with others allows you to learn from their experiences, gain fresh perspectives, and amplify your reach.

Actionable Tip: This month, reach out to one person who can offer insight or guidance for your journey. Whether it's attending a networking event, scheduling a coffee meeting with a mentor, or joining a professional group, take the first step to engage. Use this template to connect:

Hi [Name], I admire your work in [industry/role]. I'd love to learn from your journey and hear your advice. Would you be open to a brief call or coffee meeting?

Develop: Growth is Non-Negotiable

For Cathy Counselor, transitioning from high school counseling to private coaching required more than passion—it required a commitment to growth. She knew her natural ability to connect with people was a strength, but she also recognized the gaps in her knowledge. To position herself as a credible coach, Cathy enrolled in a certification program and immersed herself in learning marketing, branding, and content creation.

This investment in herself paid off. The certification gave Cathy the tools to structure her sessions effectively, while her newfound marketing skills allowed her to build a professional brand that attracted clients. By committing to continuous growth, Cathy set herself apart in a competitive market, growing her business and her confidence.

My journey with TeachTown reinforced the importance of growth. Entering the edtech space, I had to quickly learn the nuances of technology development, marketing, and scaling a business.

I immersed myself in the industry, sought guidance from seasoned experts, and committed fully to learning by doing. sought guidance from industry experts, and committed to lifelong learning. This willingness to grow wasn't optional—it was essential.

Growth is the foundation of everything you'll build. It's not about what you already know; it's about your willingness to learn, adapt, and refine your approach. Whether it's acquiring a certification, attending a workshop, or diving into self-paced online courses, investing in your skills is an investment in your future.

Actionable Tip: Identify one skill you want to develop this quarter. Enroll in a course, workshop, or webinar to strengthen that area. Platforms like LinkedIn Learning, Coursera, and Udemy offer accessible options to help you grow.

Organize: Systems Create Success

For Frida Finance, balancing her roles as a teacher, coach, and financial advisor required more than determination—it demanded organization. Frida treated her financial services career with the same professionalism as her teaching, dedicating focused blocks of time to studying, meeting clients, and refining her strategies.

She relied on systems to stay on track, using project management tools like Trello to prioritize tasks and a detailed planner to structure her day. By breaking her goals into manageable steps and staying disciplined, Frida was able to grow her financial services business while still excelling in her teaching role.

In my own journey, systems have been the backbone of success. Scaling TeachTown required meticulous planning, from setting clear priorities to delegating tasks and managing deadlines. I used systems to streamline my team's sales operations, track progress, and ensure every action aligned with our mission. Organization turned the chaos of growth into clarity, enabling me to focus on what mattered most.

Success doesn't come from working harder—it comes from working smarter. Systems aren't just tools to manage tasks—they're frameworks that keep you focused, efficient, and aligned with your goals.

Actionable Tip: Use a task manager or planner to streamline your goals into weekly action steps. Apps like Trello, Notion, or Asana can help you track progress, delegate tasks, and stay organized.

Motivate: Celebrate the Wins

For Stephanie Sped, the early days of building her school were filled with long hours, unexpected challenges, and moments of self-doubt. But she understood the importance of celebrating progress along the way. When she enrolled her first 50 students—a major milestone—she treated her team to dinner, sharing stories and gratitude for their collective effort.

Those celebrations weren't just about recognizing the milestone; they were about recharging their spirits and reminding everyone why they had embarked on this journey. Celebrating wins, no matter how small, became a source of motivation that kept Stephanie and her team focused and resilient.

In my journey, I've learned that motivation isn't something you wait for—it's something you create. At TeachTown, every milestone, whether it was a new product launch or reaching more students, was an opportunity to celebrate. These moments reinforced our mission and gave us the energy to tackle the next challenge.

Celebrating wins isn't just about rewarding yourself—it's about recognizing the progress you've made and the effort it took to get there. It keeps you connected to your purpose and builds the momentum to keep pushing forward.

Actionable Tip: Write down one way you'll reward yourself for achieving a milestone this quarter. It could be as simple as a dinner out, a day off, or investing in something that brings you joy. Celebrate every win, big or small—it's fuel for the road ahead.

EXTENDED EDUCATOR

Apply the F.R.E.E.D.O.M. Formula to Your Field

Whether you're guiding student athletes, leading a school, or helping clients heal, the F.R.E.E.D.O.M. Formula helps you grow with clarity and courage.

F.R.E.E.D.O.M. Step	Example
Focus	Define your vision. "I want to build a modern coaching program for first-gen athletes."
Reflect	What's holding you back–title, time, fear?
Evaluate	What tools, time, or training would help most?
Engage	Join a peer group. Find a business mentor. Call one person today.
Develop	Take a course. Watch a tutorial. Practice your pitch.
Organize	Use sticky notes or Notion to map out your next 30 days.
Motivate	Post your "why" where you can see it daily. Keep going!

This is your path to impact and independence—one small, intentional step at a time.

Mini-Win:

1. Write your main goal on a sticky note.
2. Break it into actionable steps (one per note).

3. Celebrate each completed step by removing a note from the board.

Reflection: F.R.E.E.D.O.M. Sticky Note Tracker

Write down one of the F.R.E.E.D.O.M. steps (Focus, Reflect, Evaluate, Engage, Develop, Organize, Motivate) you'll start implementing today. Take one action to put it into practice.

Next Chapter, New Challenge: The Final Bell

The **F.R.E.E.D.O.M. Formula** provides a clear roadmap to financial independence, but a roadmap is only as effective as the tools and systems you use to navigate it. You've equipped yourself with the tools, strategies, and mindset to step boldly into your next chapter. The systems and frameworks we've explored are designed not just to help you succeed but to empower you to redefine success on your own terms.

Now, it's time to look forward. As we move into the final chapter, we'll reflect on the growth you've experienced, the obstacles you've overcome, and the steps you've taken toward breaking free from limitations. Most importantly, we'll issue a challenge: to take the next bold step in building the life, impact, and freedom you've worked so hard to achieve.

CHAPTER 9:

The Final Bell-A Call to Action

The bell has rung its last note. No longer does it control your time, worth, or potential. You've dismantled its rhythm of limitation and replaced it with your own tempo—one of purpose, growth, and freedom.

Breaking the bell wasn't an act of rebellion—it was a declaration of your value and potential. It was a choice to believe that your skills, passions, and purpose are not bound by the confines of a classroom or any single role. The classroom may have been the starting point, but it doesn't have to define the rest of your journey.

As we close this chapter together, the question is clear: What will you do to answer the bell and move courageously into your next phase?

Reflecting on the Journey

Throughout this book, we've explored stories of courage, transformation, and bold action:

- **Pablo Principal:** As a school leader faced with financial instability and personal challenges, Pablo had to redefine his vision of leadership. He stepped out of his comfort zone and transitioned from leading a single school to influencing an entire network of educational organizations. His ability to build systems, empower others, and stay true to his purpose led him to a national leadership role, where he now drives systemic change and advocates for educational equity.
- **Frida Finance:** Frida was a middle school math teacher and coach who discovered her passion for empowering others through financial literacy. Initially overwhelmed by the idea of stepping into a world outside of education, Frida leaned into the skills she had honed in the classroom—breaking down complex concepts, building trust, and inspiring action. Today, she's thriving as a financial planner, helping families build security and achieve their goals, all while maintaining the same dedication she brought to her students.
- **Stephanie Sped:** Stephanie's journey began as a special education teacher passionate about serving students with exceptional needs. But she saw the gaps in the system and decided to create something entirely new. Despite the fears and obstacles that came with starting her own school, Stephanie founded a space where students could receive individualized support and thrive. Her perseverance turned doubt into action, and today, her school is a shining example of what's possible when educators dare to dream big.
- **Charlotte Charter:** Charlotte had a comfortable position as a principal, but her belief in creating a greater impact

drove her to build a groundbreaking charter school network. She faced countless obstacles—financial setbacks, doubters, and personal sacrifices— but her determination turned one school into a beacon of innovation.

- **Tracy Tutor:** Tracy transitioned her love for teaching and writing into a thriving business, helping students tell their unique stories through college essays. Her first steps were marked by uncertainty, but her courage to begin—even without a perfect plan—became the foundation for her success.
- **Steve Supe:** Frustrated with the stagnant education conference model, Steve built a series of conferences that redefined collaboration among educators. He showed us that innovation doesn't have to be loud—it just has to be persistent and purpose-driven.

Their stories—and yours—echo a central truth: transformation doesn't require perfection, only action. Like the bird in the open cage, breaking free is a choice. Like Andy Dufresne in *The Shawshank Redemption*[4], it may involve crawling through 500 yards of challenges, but the freedom on the other side is worth it.

Now, reflect on your journey. **What is your story? What transformation will you create?**

Answering the Bell

Breaking the bell was the first step. Answering the Bell is about taking bold, deliberate action to create the life you've envisioned. It's about putting everything you've learned—your skills, your strategies, your mindset—into practice.

Answering the bell requires embracing the discomfort of growth and trusting in your ability to build something meaningful. It means no longer waiting for ideal circumstances or permission. It's about moving forward with intention, one step at a time.

FROM Poor, Pissed-Off, and Proud
TO: Purpose, Prosperity, and Pride

For many educators, the journey begins with three emotions:

- **Poor:** Feeling undervalued and financially constrained by a system that demands so much.
- **Pissed-Off:** Frustrated by the inequities and limitations that stifle potential.
- **Proud:** Loving the work deeply and believing in its value, even when the system doesn't.

But breaking the bell transforms these emotions into something greater:

- **Purpose:** Recognizing that your skills, experiences, and passions can create meaningful change—not just for others but for yourself.
- **Prosperity:** Aligning your work with your worth, creating financial freedom and security.
- **Pride:** Living a life that honors your talents while continuing to make an impact.

What Will Your Legacy Be?

As educators, we often see our legacy in the students we teach—their growth, their successes, their futures. While that impact is profound, breaking the bell allows your legacy to extend far beyond the classroom.

By embracing change and daring to step into new opportunities, you show others what's possible. Your actions inspire those still in the cage to see the open door and step through.

Think of the stories we've shared:

- Tracy's leap into tutoring.
- Charlotte's innovative charter schools.
- Stephanie's transformative school for students with special needs.
- Pablo's rise to national leadership.
- Frida's empowering financial work.
- Steve's reimagined conferences.

Each of these individuals created a legacy of empowerment and possibility. So can you.

A Final Call to Action

The bell no longer controls your schedule, your choices, or your potential. You've taken the first steps to break free. Now, the question isn't what's holding you back—it's what you'll do with the freedom you've created.

Will your legacy be one of bold transformation, inspiring others to see their own potential? Will it be a business, a movement, or a story of personal growth that ripples outward, touching lives far beyond your own?

The beauty of breaking the bell is that the rhythm is now yours to define. You have the tools, the mindset, and the courage to build the life you've always imagined.

So I'll ask one last time: **What will your legacy be?**

The answer is entirely up to you.

EXTENDED EDUCATOR

What Will Be Said About You When the Bell Rings?

This isn't about some grand legacy. It's about how your daughters talk about you at dinner. How a former student remembers you at 28. How you feel in the quiet moments when the building is finally empty.

So many therapists, administrators, and coaches I know are haunted by the question: "Did I do enough?" But what if you flipped that script?

What if the real question is: "Did I do what I was truly called to do?"

The final bell doesn't have to mean regret—it can mean turning the page.

Write your exit plan like it's a love letter to yourself. Let your career evolve with pride, not guilt. Say what needs to be said and build what needs to be built.

Because when the final school bell rings, it isn't just the end of something—it's the echo of everything else you are destined to become.

Mini-Win:

Share your legacy statement with a trusted friend or mentor to hold yourself accountable.

Legacy Worksheet:

1. Write down one sentence about the impact you want to leave behind.
   Example: I want to be remembered as someone who inspired others to see their worth and live with purpose.
2. Identify one action you can take today to move toward that vision.
   Example: Share your story with a colleague or mentor someone on a similar path.
3. Share your legacy statement with a trusted friend or mentor to hold yourself accountable.

Closing Reflection: Answering and Breaking the Bell

The final bell has rung—but this time, it's not just a signal to move; it's a call to transform. This is your moment to not only answer the bell of opportunity but to **break the bell** that has held you back.

Imagine the bells in your life—the routines, doubts, and systems that kept you in place. Breaking these bells is the first step to answering the call of your future. You must let go of what no longer serves you and step forward with clarity, confidence, and purpose. This is how you reclaim your power, rewrite your story, and build the life you deserve.

As you move forward, remember: the skills you've honed as an educator are the foundation for endless possibilities. They've prepared you to inspire, lead, and create change—not just in others, but in yourself. By breaking the bell, you've chosen to liberate yourself from limits and embrace the limitless.

YOUR NEXT CHAPTER...

B*reaking the Bell* isn't just a book— it's a call to action for educators who are ready to own their value and step boldly into what's next.

Here's how to take the next step:

1. Get Free Resources + Weekly Boosts

   Join the **Breaking the Bell™ Newsletter** to receive:
   - Weekly strategies for life after the bell
   - Exclusive tools and templates
   - Behind-the-scenes insights
   - Early access to live coaching and course launches

   Sign up at: www.BreakingTheBell.com

2. Join the Community

   You're not alone. Connect with educators like you who are transforming their lives beyond the classroom.
   - Join the private Facebook Group: Breaking the Bell
   - Watch on YouTube:@drmanuelferrer
   - Follow on X: @thedrmanny | @breakingdbell

3. **Explore The Next Chapter™–Educator Career Transition Program:**

    The Next Chapter™–Educator Career Transition Program is your path to edupreneurship with clarity, confidence, and community. Your next move starts here.

4. **Book Your Strategy Session**

    Need personal guidance? Work one-on-one with a coach who understands both education and entrepreneurship.

    - Gain clarity
    - Build a roadmap
    - Get unstuck—fast

Book a One-on-One Strategy Session

Email us to book your strategy session at:
Book@BreakingTheBell.com

WANT HELP BREAKING THE BELL?

We offer Self-Paced, Small Group Sessions and One-on-One Coaching: Whether you're looking for personalized guidance or a supportive community of peers, I'm here to help you navigate your transition.

You don't have to figure it all out alone.

Whether you're looking for personalized one-on-one coaching or prefer the power of a small group session with like-minded educators, we've got you covered. These sessions are designed to meet you where you are—and guide you toward where you're meant to be.

Visit **www.BreakingTheBell.com** to explore coaching options, check availability, and take your next bold step.

Because your freedom is worth the investment. And your next chapter starts now.

BECOMING PART OF THE COMMUNITY

If this book has inspired you, I encourage you to join the Breaking the Bell™ community. It's a space for educators like you—visionaries who refuse to settle for less and are ready to create meaningful change. Together, we can build a network that uplifts, empowers, and transforms.

Your journey begins now. The bell no longer confines you; it frees you to dream bigger and live fully by turning the 3Ps—Poor, Pissed-Off, and Proud—into Purpose, Prosperity, and Pride.

Answer the call. Break the bell! Start your Next Chapter today!

Join our community at: **BreakingTheBell.com/Community**

SPEAKING AND MEDIA

Manuel "Dr. Manny" Ferrer, Ed.D. – National Speaker, Edupreneur, and Guest Expert

I don't just talk about change— I've helped countless educators navigate it, guiding them as they transitioned into new careers with confidence and clarity.

Over the past few years, I've had the privilege of speaking at some of the most influential education conferences and nonprofit gatherings across the country. My sessions consistently resonate because I've lived both sides of the system: as a classroom teacher and administrator, and now as a successful entrepreneur and national advocate for educator career transitions.

Topics I'm Passionate About:

- Breaking the Bell: From surviving the system to building a life of freedom
- The Next Chapter: Career transition strategies for educators ready to leap
- From Classroom to CEO: How educators can monetize their expertise
- The C4 Sales Method™: Create. Cultivate. Commit. Care. A new model for edu-sales

- AI & the Future of Educator Careers: Tools, trends, and how to stay ahead

Media & Guest Expert Appearances:

As a recognized thought leader in educator career transitions, I'm also available for:

- Podcast & TV interviews
- Guest articles & panel features
- Expert commentary on workforce reform, education-to-entrepreneur pipelines, and minority-owned business development

To request my speaker one-sheet, book an engagement, or explore media appearances email us at:

Speaking@BreakingTheBell.com

ACKNOWLEDGEMENTS

Writing this book has been one of the most personal and transformative journeys of my life. It's the product of not only my experiences, but the love, sacrifices, and encouragement of many people who believed in me long before I ever believed in myself.

To my wife, Maria:

Your faith in me has never wavered. You've walked beside me through every leap, every late night, and every chapter—literally and metaphorically. Thank you for being my partner in life and in legacy.

To my daughters, Alyssa and Bryanna:

You are the reason I strive, create, and believe in what's possible. I hope this book gives you permission to dream boldly and leap fiercely.

To the memory of my grandparents:

You gave up everything so your children and grandchildren could have a future. I am that future. Your courage lives in every page of this book.

En memoria de mis abuelos:

Lo dejaron todo atrás para que sus hijos y nietos pudieran tener un futuro. Yo soy ese futuro. Su valentía vive en cada página de este libro.

To my mother, Zoila, and my brother, Jeovanee:

Thank you for cheering me on.

To the educators I've served with:

Thank you for showing up, every day, for kids and communities—often without recognition or reward. Your stories and strength shaped the mission of Breaking the Bell.

To Cheli Grace (Book to Millions):

Thank you for your guidance, support, and encouragement through this process. Your belief in this vision helped me bring it to life with clarity and conviction.

To every school leader, district partner, and conference audience who gave me the mic:

Thank you for trusting me with your time and your educators. Your platforms gave this message wings.

To Dave Cappellucci, Wayne Hilley, and the TeachTown team:

Thank you for your mentorship, your leadership, and your belief in the power of edtech to change lives. You helped shape how I think about impact and innovation.

To my former business partners:

We may not have always agreed, but one thing we can agree on is we helped a lot of children and teachers along the way. For that, I remain grateful.

To the readers:

Whether you're reading this from the classroom, your car on lunch break, or in the quiet of a late night—you are not alone. This book was written for you, but more importantly, it was written with you in mind. Thank you for trusting me with your next chapter.

ABOUT THE AUTHOR

Manuel "Dr. Manny" Ferrer, Ed.D. is living proof that where you start doesn't define where you finish.

Raised by his grandmother in the heart of Little Havana during the height of the 1990s crack epidemic, Dr. Manny's earliest chapters were written in poverty, survival, and uncertainty. But it was education—first as a student, then as a teacher—that cracked open the door to a different life. He became the first in his family to attend college, later earning a doctorate in Educational Leadership, and returned to serve the very community that raised him.

After earning two **"Teacher of the Year"** honors and rising through the ranks to become a school administrator, Dr. Manny made a bold decision to step outside the school system. He created more for himself, his family, and the educators he knew were struggling just like he once was. From national sales executive to founder of his own education-based business, he discovered what many educators are never taught: **you don't have to sacrifice your passion to gain your freedom.**

Today, Dr. Manny is the author of **Breaking the Bell™** and the founder of **The Next Chapter™**, a career transition platform built exclusively for educators ready to reimagine their lives beyond the classroom.

Through speaking, coaching, and training programs, he now helps educators across the country design meaningful second acts—ones rooted in purpose, profit, and personal power, and reflective of his motto: **Education saved my life. Entrepreneurship set me free.**

END NOTES

1. Clarkson, Kelly. "Breakaway." *Breakaway*. RCA, 2004.
2. David Allen, *Getting Things Done: The Art of Stress-Free Productivity*. Penguin, 2015.
3. Dave Ramsey, *The Total Money Makeover: A Proven Plan for Financial Fitness*. Thomas Nelson, 2013.
4. Frank Darabont, dir., *The Shawshank Redemption* (Burbank, CA: Castle Rock Entertainment, 1994), film.

THE HYBRID SELLER™

Coming soon—get ready to break the bell and sell without limits.

Welcome to the era of modern selling.

In today's ever-evolving marketplace, old-school sales tactics aren't enough—and going fully digital isn't the answer either. The Hybrid Seller™ is your playbook for mastering the intersection of traditional relationship-building and cutting-edge digital strategy.

In this highly anticipated release, Dr. Manny Ferrer—a nationally recognized sales leader and former educator—breaks down what it truly means to sell in a post-pandemic world. Drawing from years of frontline sales leadership and training, he introduces a new kind of sales professional: agile, authentic, and unstoppable across platforms, time zones, and buyer personas.

Whether you're a sales rep looking to level up, a sales leader building a modern team, or an organization ready to future-proof your sales force, The Hybrid Seller™ delivers the frameworks, tools, and mindset you need to thrive. This isn't just a book—it's the next evolution of sales.

Be sure to email us at:
TheHybridSeller@BreakingTheBell.com to get a VIP invite to the book's release date and events.

Made in the USA
Columbia, SC
01 July 2025

305545d1-3bf6-4a1b-9057-cfcc2e103edcR01